PASSAGE
TO MANHOOD
Field Guide

CRAIG M. GLASS

What dads are saying...

The Passage to Manhood experience I shared with my son was the most impactful we have had together and marks the entry point into manhood through his understanding the characteristics of strength, heart, mind and soul. Our relationship has taken on a new meaning thanks to Craig and *Passage to Manhood*. I strongly recommend this book to any father willing to embrace vulnerability and a desire to grow in God with his son.
Boyd Williams, President and CEO, YMCA of the Pikes Peak Region

Wow! I used *Passage to Manhood* with all three of my sons when they were in high school. They each look back on that experience with fondness and as a time of truly being empowered to be the men God has called them to be. I am grateful to Craig for both the material and the experiences it helped me share with each son. I highly recommend this book to any dad who wants to call and bless his son into the manhood he was designed for.
Mike Jordahl, Senior Vice President, The Navigators

Passage to Manhood is a must read for a father who desires to be intentional about ushering his son through an important rite of passage into becoming a godly man. Going through these materials by Craig may be the single most important thing I have ever done with my son. I am so grateful that such a guide and tools are available to assist fathers who want their sons to become good men.
Vance Brown, CEO and Co-Founder, Cherwell Software

My son and I had an incredible experience at a Passage to Manhood retreat, Craig has accumulated a lot of great insights over his years of ministry that he incorporated. I believe I grew and was stretched as a father, and it created a unique relational and conversational opportunity between myself and my son that was highly impactful to him as well.
Chris Fowler, CEO, Church Community Builder

God has uniquely gifted Craig with insight into the critical aspects of men becoming authentic men; Passage to Manhood helps redeem this life-shaping concept rooted in biblical truths. My son and I went through a Passage to Manhood weekend and found it to be a powerfully bonding experience that allowed him to begin those initial steps into manhood. *Passage to Manhood* is a must-have resource and experience for every father desiring to bless his son on the journey into manhood!
Ken Sparks, CEO and President, Children's HopeChest

True to his calling, gifting and experience, Craig delivers an exceptional blueprint for fathers to lead their sons into godly and authentic manhood. This authoritative work delves deep into breaking cultural norms, the important role of the father, and the power of forgiveness and blessing. Passage to Manhood provided me a guide, language, content, and ceremony to shepherd three of my sons into manhood.
Chadd Miller, President, Glazier Clinics

Having gone through *Passage to Manhood* with two of my sons, I can say that the content is remarkable—biblically sound, expertly communicated and tremendously relevant. I give it my highest recommendation!
Dan Jensen, Ph.D., Professor of Engineering Mechanics

Passage to Manhood is a high-impact resource for any father who wants his sons to become godly, mature men. Craig blends biblical wisdom with practical exercises to help fathers and sons go deeper and further on their journey to manhood. I highly endorse and recommend Craig and *Passage to Manhood* to any father who is serious about raising a godly son.
Al Mueller, President, Excellence In Giving, LLC

Passage to Manhood was a crucial journey for my five sons and I to take together, one son at a time. Craig is a passionate leader through the topic and process of calling out sons, and we were transformed as growing Christian men. I believe in Craig, and I believe in what he is teaching men to do for their sons, a vitally necessary relationship in today's world.
Matthew E. Dealy, Co-Founder, Band of Brothers Ministry,
Executive Director, Bear Trap Ranch

Craig does an incredible job of getting fathers and sons to engage deeply around the areas of what it means to become a man. Often, fathers are not sure how to start the conversation. Not only does Craig get the conversation started, he helps navigate some of the most difficult issues confronting our sons in today's culture. Some five years later I still read to Austin the letter I wrote to him following the Passage ceremony.
David Bervig, VP of Human Resources, David C. Cook

Passage to Manhood is a great tool for a fragmented society and a fragmented family. It is a coach to help young men process what it means to become a man in their current world. I'm grateful for the opportunity for my son and I to slow down and share our stories.
Rick Clapp, Executive Pastor, Mountain Springs Church.

Passage to Manhood was one of the most impactful experiences I've had with my son. We not only spent true quality time together, we also had the opportunity to discuss powerful aspects of our family story at a level that had not been possible before. Craig helped open the door to topics that are not easy to discuss but are absolutely essential for putting young men on a course to a life that has real purpose and significance.
Steve Caton, President, The Giving Crowd

PASSAGE
TO MANHOOD
Field Guide

*Love the Lord your God with all your heart and with all your soul
and with all your mind and with all your strength…
Love your neighbor as yourself.*
Mark 12:30, 31

ACKNOWLEDGEMENTS

In 1997, a handful of men gathered together several times at the Canteen Restaurant in Barrington, IL to think through a new way of guiding young men into an understanding of their spiritual calling. The result of those meetings was a father-son rite of passage experience called Passage to Manhood.

That first step resulted in the guide you hold in your hands. I'm deeply indebted to Lew Caliento, Jim Bedell, Scott Pederson and Jim Vogelgesang, for their contributions to that project, which still bear fruit today.

This field manual served a modest, but not-entirely-fulfilled purpose for years until Mike Hamel stepped into the picture. As editor, writing coach and supportive friend, Mike guided me through the process of fulfilling this book's full potential. I'm deeply grateful to him.

Dear dads and sons,

You've made a great decision to enter into this Passage to Manhood! You are participating in a unique event that I believe will have a powerful impact on both of you.

Since biblical times fathers have passed on words of instruction and blessing to their sons. Sons have stepped into the strength and responsibility of manhood as they enter adolescence. My desire is that God instructs and inspires you both through this process and through the years that follow.

Dads, may this be a time of humility, vulnerability, courage and excitement for you. Sons, may you, like Jesus when he was young, grow "in wisdom and stature, and in favor with God and men" (Luke 2:52).

For the hearts of men.

Craig M. Glass

DEDICATION

This Field Guide is dedicated to my daughter, Barclay Kathryn, who first revealed to me the incredible joy of raising a girl; my son, Alexander McLean, who brought open-hearted willingness and wisdom to his experience of Passage as first-born son; and my son Conor Morgan, who patiently and insightfully talked through man-stuff with me over many breakfasts together. All three of you have given me immeasurable joy as your father. I love you!

My deep gratitude also goes to my wife, Beryl, who not only lovingly and faithfully supported me every step of the way in developing the *Passage to Manhood Field Guide*, but contributed her remarkable gifts as graphic design artist of this book. I love you too!

PASSAGE
TO MANHOOD

CONTENTS

Welcome to Passage to Manhood 11

I. Strength: The Courage of a Warrior 17

The Value of Work, Adversity and Challenge 23

Rejecting Shame 31

Living in Purity 39

Covenant of Commitment and Support 45

II. Heart: The Compassion of a Lover 47

Admitting and Healing Wounds 51

Family Story Exercise 59

Honoring Women 63

III. Mind: The Conviction of a Mentor 69

Building Character 73

Building a Band of Brothers 77

IV. Soul: The Confidence of a King 83

God Rules 89

Jesus Saves 95

Discovering Your Mission 99

Celebration Ceremony 107

Passage Certificate 110

Father/Son Adventure 111

 ## WELCOME TO PASSAGE TO MANHOOD

OK, sons, I can almost hear you thinking, "What in the world has my dad gotten me into? This Passage thing seems weird; I don't get it."

That's exactly right, we don't get it. We're going to be talking about what it means to be man; a topic that is rarely discussed these days. But the truth is, most men really want to know, *what does it take to be a man?* Because nothing is more important to men than knowing they fit and that they are in "the club"— a fraternity of men. As one saying puts it, "It takes a man to tell a man he's a man."

So what is a man? That's a question that rarely would have been asked 120 or more years ago. But since then, changes in our society have transformed the roles that men have traditionally filled, and that has often blurred the distinctions between men and women to the point that it's hard to know what is different, other than our physical distinctions.

In most cultures throughout history, men taught their sons by example, living in the home, working together, giving the son skills and a trade that he could carry on. Roles acted out by women and men were usually distinct. Men tended to work the farm, work a trade, work in a factory, pursuing employment in or outside the home that provided for financial needs.

Women tended to do more of the work within the home, spending more time teaching or raising the children during the day. Women usually prepared meals and cared for the upkeep of the home. For generations, in most cultures around the world, those roles remained largely the same.

Until relatively recently. In the lifetime of your grandparents, traditional roles played by men and women have changed dramatically. Many women now work outside the home. Today it's just as common for the financial needs of a family to be provided by the mother as by the father. Some fathers are stay-at-home dads and care for the home and children during the day.

These changes have brought a needed sharing of responsibilities and greater freedom for women to pursue their own gifts and education. That has had a very positive effect for women, and for many businesses. But those changes have also brought an assumption that there are no differences between men and women.

Due to a dramatic increase in divorce rates and the demands of industrialized workplaces, families have become much more disjointed than they were even a generation ago. Dads usually work in settings separated from family exposure; the great majority work in complete isolation from their children. Boys have no clue what their dad does; nor do they know what goes on in their dad's life other than what sports he likes or lame TV shows he watches.

As a result boys in our society frequently receive very little input as to the uniqueness of being a man, how men are different than women, and what they might dream of becoming as they grow into masculinity. Our society largely implies that becoming a man means you can now drink alcohol, smoke tobacco, go to war and buy pornography. Congratulations, you're a man; you now get to hurt yourself! While allowing for these "rites of passage," society does very little to prepare boys for the momentous responsibilities and consequences they entail. Some boys may be ready to handle these decisions; many aren't.

Deep down inside, boys suspect there should be more than this simple, coincidental permission to explore danger that depends on nothing other than their birthdate. Teenage boys may not fully realize it, but they long for meaning, for manly companionship, for some kind of adventure to live. Boys want to belong to a group of men that represents a larger "story" or challenge.

For some teens a sports team, a jazz band, the Boy Scouts, or the military satisfies that longing. All of those offer some kind challenge, and a generally positive one, that helps a boy feel like men accept him.

But sadly, for many boys there is nothing intentional or healthy that communicates the message to them that "they matter." As a result, they create their own men's rites of passage groups. For some boys that longing is superficially fulfilled through the "adventure" of video games, which offer thrills, challenge, combat, competition, and "victory." But, because the challenge is largely virtual, in other words unreal, the victory and affirmation they promise are also limited. Like sexual pornography that promises, but can't fully deliver genuine relational intimacy, video games cannot deliver genuine affirmation of accomplishment. They're adventure porn.

> Love God with all your heart, soul, mind and strength

Many other teenage boys on the prowl for manly affirmation take a more dangerous path that tells them they matter. They're called gangs. Gangs are a natural result of the God-given desire young men have to belong, to be "seen" by other men and to be significant. An older boy tells a young one he'll be considered a man if he wears a certain color, knocks over a 7-Eleven or shoots a guy from another block. With no other manly voice that tells him the passage rules, that young boy will do whatever it takes.

Young men in American gangs are fulfilling the very same Kenyan proverb that fits African societies, "The boys in the village must be initiated into manhood…or they will burn down the village, just to feel the heat." With no positive options in which to direct their energy, boys turn to destruction.

Are the above options all there are for boys to learn what it means to be manly? Your dad doesn't think so. He thinks it's time we taught our sons that being a man is an honorable thing. He's taking a courageous step to invite you into this journey. It's courageous on his part because virtually no men in Western societies, or even the Christian community, do this any more. Dads and sons in Jesus' culture took this journey. So did African and Native American cultures, along with many others. Ours doesn't.

In today's world we have largely lost the formal traditions of initiation into manhood. Instead, even adult men are confused about what it means to be a true man, and they don't know how to guide their sons in a clear way to achieve manhood.

Over a lifetime, boys without direction and guidance become men who hide doubts that they measure up to manhood. They have little idea of what exactly to pass on to their sons. Not long ago I sat in a room with about 40 men spanning the ages of 18-49. When they were asked, "What does it mean to be a man?" they sat in silent ignorance. Some eventually offered vague descriptions like, "He's strong," or "He wears the pants in the family," or "He's the one who shaves."

When it comes to a community of Christ-following men intentionally walking with their sons into an understanding and blessing of godly manhood, our culture remains largely silent. As one author puts it, "What remains silent in the father, lives in the son." Secret wounds and sins in a father's life will be passed on. Blessing will stay dormant.

This is a courageous step for your dad because he's walking in the dark, just like you. In almost all cases, this journey is as new to him as it is to you. He is largely unaware of what we will talk about, what he will be asked to say or do. But he is stepping forward. He's being a man.

So, we are asking you to be a man, too. Step into this even though it's a little scary. Trust your dad; trust the process. Be open to what this experience may have in store for you. We will respect you and honor your opinions. We will especially respect your feelings; they are welcome here. I'm asking you to do the same for your dad. Are you willing to do that?

I hope so. This will be an experience like none you've had before. We will tell stories, watch video clips, hear truth from Scripture, engage in fun adventure and learn together what God had in mind for you when he made you a man.

In particular we will look at the life of Jesus and listen to his teaching. We will explore four main characteristics of godly manliness that paint a clear picture of what true manhood looks like. These four areas will serve as the framework we will use to teach the ways of manhood.

What does it look like to be a man? We can get a clear idea of what Jesus thought by examining his response to a very difficult question, "Of all the commandments, which is the most important?" Jesus said simply, "Love the Lord your God with all your heart, with all your soul, with all your mind and with all your strength…love your neighbor as yourself" (Mark 12:30, 31).

In two sentences he not only fully answered a spiritual riddle thrown at him, he revealed how God has designed men and women: with heart (emotions), soul (spirit), mind (intellect) and strength (body). That covers everything; there isn't anything else about us other than these four aspects.

I see a corresponding characteristic for each of the four components referred to in Mark 12:30 that defines godly manhood: Compassion, Confidence, Conviction and Courage. I also find it helpful to picture a corresponding image that illustrates the various roles men live out: Lover, King, Mentor and Warrior.

Here are the correlations as I see them:
- Heart – Compassion – Lover
- Soul – Confidence – King
- Mind – Conviction – Mentor
- Strength – Courage – Warrior

In this field guide I'll present them in a slightly different order than they appear in the passage. This is primarily because it's easier for men to understand the whole picture by entering through the Warrior door, which intuitively sounds manly, than it is through the Lover door, which may sound feminine, though it is absolutely a manly quality.

All these components are guided by the biblical truth of doing what honors God and what benefits others. Men who develop each of these characteristics are truly becoming godly men. The Passage to Manhood is not the culmination of this process; rather, it is a significant milestone when a father and son explore these truths together, marking a profound step in a journey that will continue the rest of their lives.

Welcome to the journey.

 # I. STRENGTH: The Courage of a Warrior

When men "love God and others with all of their strength" the quality that rises to the surface is *Courage*. Truly courageous men know that courage is not the absence of fear; it is the willingness to enter fear. It is the commitment to act even when we are uncertain of the outcome.

Courageous men take action in order to defend: 1). Principles they believe in, and, 2). People they love. They are willing to stand against threats to their integrity and threats to their family and friends. They may not know what the consequence of their courage will be, but they are still willing to act. And they are willing to face the ridicule, rejection and even failure that might come their way.

Young men of courage reject the pressure of friends who try to get them to use drugs or alcohol in order to be accepted. Rather than giving in to the temptation to bully another student, they stand by the side of those being bullied. They have a toughness that allows them to stand strong and defend what is right.

Older men of courage take a similar stand at work or at home when they are tempted to compromise their integrity, treat a colleague or family member unfairly, or cut corners in order to make more money.

Truly courageous men do not give in to pressure or to pain. They can "fight the good fight of faith" (1 Timothy 6:12) with perseverance and endurance. They have strength that comes from within, rather than the bluster and posing that we see from those whose primary emotion is anger.

Ultimately men of courage know that the toughest battles we will ever fight on earth are against an unseen enemy. Ephesians 6:10-12 tells us that our battle is not against flesh and blood, but against spiritual powers that influence flesh and blood. It is the Enemy, who looks for any victims he can harm and destroy, who is the force behind our greatest battles. In a spiritual battle we must take our courage and strength from the Holy Spirit who lives in us.

The image that best fits a man of courage is a *Warrior*. Throughout history as well as literature, a warrior had courage and faced fear.

He went to battle, often for his king, to fight against threats to his kingdom and family. Of course he was afraid, but he did not give in to fear. Instead he got encouragement from fellow warriors who helped him to stand strong.

In the Bible, David was a warrior. He had a great sense of conviction that his cause was right, that God was with him and would strengthen him. He stood strong and courageous before Goliath, the most feared fighter among his enemies. It was courage that allowed David to face his fear and act victoriously.

Men of courage stand strong and resist what is wrong. Jesus was a courageous warrior when he drove out the moneychangers in the temple. He was so convinced that he was right that he stood up for the purity of the temple. He used anger in a good way, to stand against what was wrong.

Even today men of courage know what is right and act on it no matter how afraid they might be or what the cost might be. Remember, courageous men take action in order to defend principles they believe in and people they love.

A characteristic to remember for men of courage is: **They get in the way**. When Eve was threatened and confused by Satan in the Garden of Eden, she needed Adam to step up and get in the way, to stand between her and a threat. He didn't. Men have unfortunately behaved in this same fearful, passive way ever since.

A principle to remember about men of courage: They get in the way

When men see co-workers being mistreated at work, they need to get in the way, and push for fairness. When dads see their children being misled by the values of the world, they need to get in the way and speak truth. When sons watch a friend being bullied at school, they need to get in the way and stand up for those who might be weaker.

Remember, courage is not the absence of fear; courage is the willingness to engage fear, and then act. Real men, godly men, have the Courage of a Warrior.

Bible passages to read together:
>**Joshua 1:6-9** - Be strong and courageous
>**I Samuel 17** - David and Goliath
>**Matthew 21:12-17** - Jesus turns the tables
>**Matthew 26:36-46** - Jesus faces crucifixion and betrayal
>**John 8:1-11** - Jesus defends a woman from being killed
>**Ephesians 6:10-18** - Our battle is against unseen powers

Movie to watch together:
>*Braveheart* (Especially scene 20, Freedom!)

Dads, in all my movie recommendations, I've highlighted scenes that best illustrate my points and are also appropriate for teenagers. I don't, however, endorse every scene in every movie listed here, and urge you to use your own discretion in choosing what you watch together.

DISCUSSION QUESTIONS

Dad and Son:

1. What is one of the most courageous things you've ever had to do? Why did it take courage for you to do it?

2. Can you think of a time when you fought for someone or something that was important to you? What or who was it?

3. Have you ever been rejected or teased for not going along with the crowd?

Read Ephesians 6:10-18.

4. When have you experienced this unseen battle that is so common to men?

5. How can you each pray for and support the other to be a Courageous Warrior?

Dad:
1. How courageous was your dad? When did you see him stand up for what was right?

2. The unhealthy extremes of men are the rage-filled man who attacks others out of his own pain, or the fearful or passive man who cannot express anger and strength at all. What kind of man was your dad?

3. Was his anger based on his sense of justice or was it rage about his own personal needs not getting met? If he was passive, how did that make you feel?

4. Have you picked up any of your dad's anger or fear?

Son:
1. When have you seen your dad being courageous? How did that make you feel about him?

2. How have you seen your dad express anger? What kinds of things make him angry? Does his anger sometimes feel unjust or unfair?

3. Have you picked up any of your grandfather's or father's fear or anger? In what ways?

4. What requires the most courage from you at home or school?

(Author's note: I'm indebted to Scott Pederson, a former Willow Creek staff member, for much of the content in the following section.)

THE VALUE OF WORK, ADVERSITY AND CHALLENGES

WORK. It's not a pleasant word or thought in the opinion of many, if not most, people. It seems like a necessary evil, a four-letter word or a curse of some kind. People spend a lot of time trying to figure out how they can reduce the amount of work they must do or thinking of ways they can get out of doing it completely. Whether it is the chores around the house, the assignments from school, the labors in the office or construction site, the workouts for the athletic team, or flipping burgers at the corner fast food restaurant. We would much rather play, relax, hang out, veg, drop out or punch out than work.

Excuses abound when conversations turn to the issue of work, accompanied by whining, complaining attitudes, finger pointing and choice words. Every week at convenience stores millions of people lay down their money along with a card bearing scratch marks next to some numbers in the hope that the numbers they choose will win them enough money so they can quit work, eliminate this curse from their lives and then just float through their remaining days.

Is work a punishment dealt out by God because of sin?

What about it…is work a curse? Is work a punishment dealt out by God upon the entire human race because of the sin and disobedience of the first man and woman, Adam and Eve? Is work God's curse or his design? Would work still exist had sin never entered the scene? Or are there value, purpose and benefit to work.

Let's consider what the Bible has to say about this subject since it reveals God's intentions and his character.

From the opening sentences of Genesis, the first book of the Bible, we see God in action. "In the beginning God created…" From the very start we see God putting forth effort, and from the repeated comment, "and he saw that it was good", we can be assured that he was pleased with the results. God's example of work, and well-done work, is an illustration of the importance he places on quality effort. From the beginning, work was part of God's design by example.

We continue to see God's intention regarding work as we read on in the first chapter of Genesis. Genesis 1:28 says, "And God blessed them (Adam and Eve) and told them, 'Multiply and fill the earth and subdue it; you are masters of the fish and birds and all the animals…'" and Genesis 2:15, "Then God placed the man in the Garden of Eden as its gardener, to tend and care for it" (The Living Bible).

From these scriptures we are informed that God had a job waiting for the first couple: "Take care of my creation." It was not that God was incapable of caring for what he had made, but rather that he wanted to bless Adam and Eve by sharing this opportunity with them. And, yes, it would require work. Perhaps the first physical work ever done by humans was gardening and landscaping.

There are at least three truths we can take away from Genesis 1:28 and 2:15:
1. that God blessed the man and woman
2. that God assigned some important purposeful work in the garden
3. that man was given dominion and responsibility for the animals

Work was not a punishment; rather, work gave purpose to the man and woman.

There is one more truth regarding human labor as it relates to "the Fall" or the sin of Adam and Eve. We can read one of the consequences of this act of disobedience in Genesis 3:17-19, And to Adam, God said, "Because you listened to your wife and ate the fruit when I told you not to, I have placed a curse on the soil. All your life you will struggle to extract a living from it. It will grow thorns and thistles for you, and you shall eat grasses. All your life you will sweat to master it, until your dying day."

In one act of disobedience, the beauty of God's plan regarding work was entirely altered. Now work would be difficult, hard and sweaty, even painful. Yet, in spite of this awful change in God's original design of work, he still presents to us the privilege of meaningful labor and the benefits it provides to each of us.

What are some of those benefits?
- increased confidence and self-esteem
- strengthened character
- experiencing moments of accomplishment
- contributing to a cause
- earning an honest wage
- providing for self and family
- having a purpose
- developing and improving abilities

The benefits of work are numerous, yet people tend to dwell on the negatives. The truth is, all of us want to have meaning in our lives. Work and labor, acts of contributing to our world, add to purpose in life. There are not too many things more depressing to see than somebody who is not doing anything with their life.

Many people are discontent, even unhappy, with their daily job. This does not mean that work therefore is a bad idea. What it does mean is that perhaps a change in attitude is needed. While realizing that there will always be aspects of work that are difficult, we are still are responsible to get it done.

This goes for daily chores around the house as well as in the career we have chosen. The parts of our work that we find satisfying, even enjoyable, create job satisfaction. The aspects of our work that we wrestle with can help us develop new abilities as well as strengthen character.

Son, the fact is, work is not going to go away in this world, and leeching off of society is not an alternative to work. As a young man it is not too early to contribute to your family by taking on work assignments around the house, doing your chores without complaining, doing the best job you can do and even getting a part-time job to earn some spending money. It is also not too soon to begin thinking about what your interests are and what kind of work you could see turning into a career.

Through adversity we recognize our need for God

Some questions, dad: What perception of work is your son getting from you? What does your son know about your work? Are your conversations about work encouraging to your son or are they more negative in nature? Does your work ethic reflect the type of standard you would like your son to adopt?

ADVERSITY
Another reality of life is what we will call ADVERSITY. The Webster Dictionary defines adversity as "Great affliction or hardship."

Obviously nobody would wish adversity on another person nor does anybody want adversity to visit their life. Yet, we all know that adversity will be part of life. No doubt each of us has already experienced the sting of adversity even as a teenager.
What are the positives of adversity? One is that we are reminded that we are unable to really control any aspect of our lives. We can dream, plan, set goals and take action. Some dreams will become reality, some will not. The fact is, we will experience sadness, dis-

appointments, failures, sickness, loss and a variety of other life realities that will fall under the category of adversity.

Adversity was not part of God's original plan. Rather it is one of the results of the "Fall," or the "original sin" of Adam and Eve, that will create complications for all of us throughout life. Still, even adversity can provide moments of growth (even though painful), development of character, courage, perseverance and the ability to empathize with others (Romans 5:3, 4).

It also can bring us to the truth that we need God's involvement in our lives. Yes, we may get angry at God for allowing adversity to invade our lives and we may even blame him for it, but the end result is that it is in adversity that we recognize just how weak we are, how little control we have in life, and that we need God.

As we grow in age, experience, and maturity we will become well acquainted with adversity and our lives will be shaped in part by our response to the adversity. Some people will shake their fists at God and cry, "Why me?" while others will feel the pain, come to God and whisper, "Help me."

CHALLENGES

There is yet one more aspect to growing up that we must look at. (Hopefully you are not getting too overwhelmed at this point.) This reality of growing up toward and throughout manhood is the subject of CHALLENGES.

Actually, your life has already been full of challenges since birth. Learning to walk, to talk, to play, to read, to study, to dress yourself, to share, to write, to ride a bike, to swim, to play an instrument, etc. Everything that you have learned has been a challenge, even if some have come easier than others. You know that your life will be made up of one challenge after another. Some will be dictated by life while others will be chosen.

Regardless of how the challenges of your life come about, you will be faced with a choice. Will you face this challenge, or will you walk or even run away from it? The challenges you face will shape, in part, the kind of person you will become. Challenges will teach you courage, the art of facing fears and identifying weaknesses. Facing them will provide opportunities to experience successes as well as failures, both of which provide many life lessons.

There are all kinds of slogans in our faces these days that try to convince us that being number one is all there is. Anything else and we are losers. Even Olympics silver medal winners are sometimes called the First Loser. What a lie! There doesn't seem to be any room for the willingness to take on a challenge and do our best regardless of the place we finish.

When a person takes a challenge, he or she is saying, "I will not give up, I'll do my best, and I'll learn from the experience," regardless of whether it's athletic challenge, scholastic challenge, relational challenge, occupational challenge, or spiritual challenge. Challenges provide opportunities for personal growth. We will be very boring unfulfilled people, and we will miss out on so much of life, if we avoid challenges.

Bible passages to read together:
> **Psalms 71:20, 21** - Though we may struggle, God will restore us
> **Proverbs 12:9, 11** - The wise man works had to provide food
> **Proverbs 14: 23** - Work hard; don't just talk
> **Proverbs 21:25, 26** - Lazy men become selfish
> **Romans 5:3, 4** - Adversity produces character
> **Galatians 6:4, 5** - Men should fulfill their own responsibilities, not worry about others
> **Galatians 6:7-10** - We will receive according to what we have invested
> **1 Timothy 5:8** - We are to provide for our family
> **James 1:2-4** - Trials produce maturity

Movie to watch together:
> *City Slickers*

DISCUSSION QUESTIONS

Dad:

Tell your son about your first job. Go into detail. How old were you? How did you get that job? Why did you choose it? What were your responsibilities? How long did you work on that job? What was your boss like? What was your salary? What did you like about it? What did you dislike about it? What did you learn while on that job? What did you do with the money you earned?

Son:

What do you do around your house that contributes to making the household run smoothly? What is your general attitude? How many times do you need to be reminded to do your work? What would you say your work quality is on a scale of one to ten (with 10 being excellent)?

Based upon what you hear your dad say about his job and what you see in his actions as they relate to his work, what have you learned about the value of work? (Ouch!)

Dad:

Tell your son about some of the adversity that you have faced in your life. Be honest about it. Not just the surface level stuff. Open your life, and your heart to your son. How have you handled some of your adversity, both positive and negative? What have the results been?

Son:

What is one area of adversity that you have been facing alone because you are afraid to talk to your dad about it or you are too embarrassed to discuss it with your dad?

Talk about challenges you are facing right now, then talk about how you can face the challenges together.

 ## Rejecting Shame

One of the most awful forces in the world is Shame. It is one of the main ways Satan, the Enemy, tries to destroy both men and women. We are told in Scripture that he does this in I Peter 5:8: "Your enemy the devil prowls around like a roaring lion looking for someone to devour."

Shame is one of the primary ways the Enemy looks to devour Christ-followers. Here is what we mean by shame, starting with what it isn't:

1. **Shame is not just a lack of decency.** Our use of the word shame is not the way it has commonly been used to describe public decency, or a sense of decorum. We have a way of using the word that actually is an appropriate emotion to feel:

It is said that young people today are shameless. What they mean is that some young people (some old ones, too) have no sense of what is appropriate public behavior or dress. "They have no shame."

Some business people who incorporate shady practices to steal wealth from others "have no shame." They take enormous advantage of people who trust them with power and wealth, and then betray those same people by using that power for their own good only.

It's true; in many cases there are people who have no sense of shame; a lack of decency.

2. **Shame is not the same as guilt; in fact, it is far from it.** Guilt is about behavior; it's black and white. We're either guilty of a certain action or we're innocent. It is true of us.

If we are caught in a lie, or stealing, or cheating at school or work, we are simply guilty. Though we might try to justify or lie our way out, there is no honest arguing about the behavior. The Holy Spirit convicts us of our guilt. And God forgives us. The price is paid; the sin is gone from God's memory as far as the east is from the west.

Shame is unlike guilt in just about every way. It is not based on *external behavior*, it is an attack on *internal identity*. It is not clearly *black and white*, it is enshrouded in a *gray haze* that we are often blind to.

It is full, not of *conviction*, but of *condemnation*. Far from being *the truth*, it is a *lie about us*. And the primary voice is not from the *Holy Spirit*; the primary voice is from *Satan himself*.

WHAT SHAME IS

In his outstanding book, *Shame and Grace* (which serves as a key source for many of these insights) Lewis Smedes, a former professor at Fuller School of Theology, says:

Shame is a very heavy feeling that we don't measure up…The feeling of shame is about our very selves not about something bad we said or did but about who we are. It tells us that we are unworthy. Totally.

It is the belief that, if others know the truth about me, they will abandon and reject me. At its core, that message is a lie. But we believe it's the truth. We are hopelessly defective.

If you scratch beneath the surface of just about any self-protective or sinful behavior, you'll find shame. Shame is the heavy mask that covers our doubt of the value of our identity in Christ. We hide our shame behind numerous masks such as perfectionism, workaholism, intimidation, control, passivity, violence and addictive behavior.

Shame is both the source and the consequence of our sin. We choose to rely on selfish or harmful behavior to satisfy the pain of shame rather than accepting who God sees us as being. We sin by harming others, numbing ourselves, and by compensating through performance. We get short-term relief, but long-term…shame. Soon we want to fill the void again. And on it goes.

We think we're the only ones like us and no one must know; least of all any other Christians. And the Enemy loves it, he laughs, he rolls his hands together and celebrates this dark cycle.

THE SOURCES OF SHAME

1. The Fall in the Garden of Eden. In the grand scheme of things shame entered the biblical picture at the very beginning, when Adam and Eve betrayed God's trust in them by eating the fruit he told them not to.

Genesis 3 tells us that they immediately noticed they were naked and they covered themselves up. It's like they realized, "I am now exposed for others to see. There is something about me now that must be hidden, even from God's eyes."

When God called to them they hid themselves because they were ashamed. And once he encounters them with the question of what they have done, they respond with shame-soaked excuses:

Adam: "The woman you put here with me—she gave me some fruit..." Essentially he says, "It's her. She's to blame...and truth be told, God, even you are partly at fault for giving her to me." His excuse is even lamer than the original sin.

Eve is no better: "The serpent deceived me."
Adam says, "The woman made me do it." Eve says, "The devil made me do it."

In response, they protect, hide, blame and cover up. And with that encounter shame came to every man and woman.

That is the root of shame, but as Smedes tells us, there are more familiar sources.

2. *Secular culture.* All we have to do is watch TV commercials for two hours in primetime and we will see a series of subtle sales driven messages that are, at there heart, shame-filled. "What you have, what you own, where you live, what you drive, how you look, how you dress, how you smell, simply does not measure up. There is something wrong with virtually everything about you. You fall short of our culture's minimum standards." Shame on you.

> A person can catch a healthy case of shame in church

3. *Graceless religion.* In their encouragement of a Christ-like lifestyle many churches pass on a message that is more about performance than it is about grace. Many young people, and adults, become convinced that they must impress other Christians and God in order to be worthy of his acceptance. Smedes says, "A person can catch a healthy case of shame in church."

4. *Unaccepting parents.* Many parents raise their kids with an attitude that demonstrates that they are more concerned that their son or daughter's behavior reflects well on them, than they are in discovering how God has uniquely made their child—even if he is very different—and then celebrating those differences. How many times have parents said to their kids, "I'm ashamed of you. You should be ashamed of yourself." The wound of those words goes right to the heart of a child's self-worth.

5. *The Enemy.* The seeds of our shame begin in the Garden; those seeds are planted and watered by our secular culture, by grace-less churches and unaccepting parents. But the true nurturer of our shame is the Enemy himself.

He takes that seed and covers it in the dark soil of hiddenness, and fertilizes it with self-condemnation until it grows into a weed that wraps around us and clings to our view of ourselves. He takes our guilt, convinces us that, though it may be forgiven we are still defective because our sin is darker than anyone else's. If found out we will be rejected and abandoned by those who mean the most to us.

HEALING OUR SHAME

1. *We embrace grace.* The beginning of healing from shame is understanding that: "We are accepted by the Grace of the One whose acceptance of us matters most," says Smedes. Dads and sons, you are not only forgiven, you are accepted by the One whose acceptance lasts for eternity. Never to be rejected or abandoned. That's it; that's all; that's enough. Or it should be enough, but sadly, sometimes shame returns.

2. *We believe what God says about forgiveness and acceptance.* We need to soak ourselves with the truth of God's words about us. Hebrews 10:17,18 say, "Their sinless and unlawful acts I will remember no more. And where these have been forgiven there is no longer any sacrifice for sin!" Psalm 103:11-13 tells us God has tossed our sins as far away as possible from his sight.

3. *We believe what God's word says about shame.* Romans 8:1 says, "Therefore, there is now no condemnation for those who are in Christ Jesus." Conviction? Sure. That comes from the Holy Spirit; it's conviction about our behavior. That gets forgiven and forgotten.

Condemnation? None. Condemnation attacks our value and worth; it comes from the Enemy, and it's a lie from the pit of hell.

Psalm 25:3 says, "No one whose hope is in you will ever be put to shame..." Look at those words, "No one," "ever." They are pretty inclusive. And Psalm 34: 4 and 5 says, "I sought the Lord and he answered me; he delivered me from all my fears. Those who look to him are radiant; their faces are never covered with shame." But sadly, sometimes reminding ourselves of the truth in God's word isn't enough. Shame returns. Then what?

4. **We bring trusted friends into the journey.** I John 1:7 says, "But if we walk in the light, as he is in the light, we have fellowship with one another, and the blood of Jesus, his Son, purifies us from all sin." When we walk openly with a few trusted friends, in the light, we not only experience brotherhood with them, we experience spiritual transformation.

5. **We renounce shame.** *Repeatedly, verbally.* That means out loud so Satan hears it. There is no reason the enemy shouldn't continue his attacks on us. In the same way, there is no reason for us to hesitate to pray against them.

Shame becomes like a cloak around us. It has taken years to collect it. It may take years to finally be freed of it. It has become so conformed to us that sometimes we think it IS us. It's not. We must pray that God removes it, separates us from it. Takes it away and burns it in the trash heap it belongs in.

Bible passages to read together:
Genesis 3 - Shame entered men's lives in the Garden of Eden
Psalm 25:1-3 - No one who hopes in God will be put to shame
Psalm 34: 4, 5 - Those who look to God are not shamed
Psalm 103:11, 12 - God removes our sin forever
Romans 8:1-4 - There is no condemnation for Christ-followers
Hebrews 10:17, 18 - God doesn't even remember our sins
I Peter 5:8, 9 - The devil wants to destroy us
I John 1:7 - Walk in the light with other men

Movie to watch together:
The Mission (Especially the scene entitled Redemption)

DISCUSSION QUESTIONS

Dad and Son:

1. Can both of you come up with an example of a time when you acted in a sinful way, but were (or still are) uncertain whether it has been completely forgiven? Tell each other the story.

2. We hide our shame behind numerous masks. Which of these responses might be true of how you handle shame?

   • We become perfectionists: deep inside we have flaws we want to cover up.
   • We become workaholics: compensating for a lack of worth by pursuing success.
   • We intimidate others with anger and violence: lest they see our fear or weakness.
   • We retreat into passivity: taking no chance that we might fail once again.
   • We pursue addictive behavior: to comfort and quiet the voices of condemnation.

3. How would you feel about telling another Christian about the experience you thought of in question 1, or your answer to question 2? Do you have a friend or group of friends who you can tell the truth to, and know you'll be accepted? If so, how did you get this group? If not, how can you find a friend like this?

Reread the verses in Psalms and Romans above and pray out loud for each other.

(Author's note: I'm indebted to Jim Bedell, a friend and experienced clinical psychologist, for much of the content in this section and the section on Honoring Women.)

 ## LIVING IN PURITY

The true man of God is urged to demonstrate control over his body so that he is not dominated by the attraction of lust. Why is that so important to God? Is it because God is somehow a mean-spirited judge who loves to frustrate human pleasure?

No—God has created us to experience pleasure. But he wants us to experience pleasure and fulfillment within the discipline of healthy relationships defined by commitment.

Given our self-centered sinfulness, we naturally try to gain personal pleasure at the expense of others. The end result is a tendency to use others to meet our needs, which results in damaged relationships. With the power of Christ at work in us, we have the ability to honor others rather than use them for our own pleasure. In practice, this means we grow in our ability to love; we reduce our tendency to selfishly meet the demands of our longings at the expense of others.

In 1 Thessalonians 4:3-8, Paul calls believers to live a life that is pleasing to God. Essentially, this is a life that is submitted to God and to getting one's needs met in an honorable and balanced way. We are called to avoid sexual immorality, to learn to control our bodies in honorable ways (1 Corinthians 6:18-20).

Paul disciplined his body for the higher purpose of being in a place where the vulnerability to temptation did not side track him from his higher mission (1 Corinthians 9:24-27). Spiritual maturity is the ability to choose to love from an other-focused heart, not a heart driven by self-centered interest. To do this, we have to put away the lusts of the flesh.

Purity is a concept related to the science of metal composition. Pure metals have no "dross," or material that weakens the strength of the metal. Any impurity in a metal makes it vulnerable to stress fractures and weakens the quality of the metal. Pure gold was a highly valued commodity throughout Bible times. The purity of the metal was critical so that nothing diluted its strength.

The Bible uses the concept of purity to refer to the same principle of diluting the strength of a man's commitment. The man with a pure heart has removed the "dross" of competing interests so that he is strong in his commitment to God. On the other hand, impurity (especially sexual impurity) dilutes the strength of a man in many ways:

1. **Delaying maturity.** Sexual impurity weakens a man's ability to grow and mature. Early on, as a boy, thoughts of sexuality create pleasurable feelings and excitement. If a boy masturbates, he feels a rush of pleasure that comes when he experiences orgasm. The memory of this sensation is very intense for boys, and men, and can become an experience that they want to have often.

Sexual thoughts and feelings produce a chemical change in the body and brain that is pleasurable, and so can be addictive and pre-occupying. Since boys and men have a great deal of difficulty in handling painful feelings such as sadness, fear, loneliness, and hurt, the thought of sex can help them escape these negative feelings. As a result, they may not learn more constructive ways to cope with these real human emotions, such as bringing them to God or to other Christian men for encouragement and support. Instead, sexual fantasies or masturbation can become a selfish, and even childish, way that men comfort themselves in their loneliness.

2. **Demeaning women.** Most boys, at some point, struggle to separate from their moms. This is a natural part of growth. When separation doesn't happen in a healthy way—negative results can take place. Sometimes, in order for a son to separate from his mom, he begins to view her as an inferior person. This is especially true if he has seen this example in his father or older men around him. The son may generalize this condescending attitude toward women as a whole, and this may result in his reducing women to a role of servitude to men.

In the sexual area, this can result in men seeing women only as sources of pleasure. The spiritual, intellectual, and emotional dimensions of women are ignored. They are diminished and assumed to be less than the man. This is inconsistent with the way that God views women as equal to men in worth and value (Galatians 3:26-29). Men are called to honor the women in their lives not to view them solely as objects for lust or self-satisfaction.

3. **Destroying trust.** There is no greater requirement for a healthy relationship with another person than the element of trust. Trust conveys to another that they are safe with you and can reveal their needs and fears. The most important element in creating trust in a romantic relationship is demonstrating to your partner that you are a person that has enough self-discipline to delay your personal satisfaction when it ignores the needs of your partner.

A person who is sexually impure acts in a way that is focused on meeting his own needs, no matter what the consequences to their partner may be. The man that masturbates in secret or is intimate with someone other than his wife is not a man who his partner can trust. He is not able to say "No" to his own needs in favor of his partner's.

The man who has brought his sexual urges under discipline is a man who is trustworthy and safe to his wife. She can count on that man to not hurt her just to gratify his own needs. In the book of Proverbs, many times men are called to not give in to the lure of a seductive woman or prostitute. The prostitute, or any promiscuous woman, calls and promises to gratify the immediate needs of the man, but she does not reveal that the outcome afterward is a deep sense of shame.

Proverbs 23:27, 28 says, "…for a prostitute is a deep pit and a wayward wife is a narrow well. Like a bandit she lies in wait, and multiplies the unfaithful among men." Men who are sexually impure are ultimately untrustworthy; they do not create a confidence that they will protect the vulnerability that their partner offers to them.

4. **Diminishing power.** Ironically, although men who are sexually active like to boast about their conquests over women, the reality is that they are ultimately impotent. (Impotence is a sense of deep powerlessness or inability to control something.) Impotency in this situation relates to the fact that men who are impure are often trapped by their own inability to say "no" to sexual temptation, even when it is harmful to their spiritual and relational growth and fulfillment.

The sexually preoccupied man does not feel like he has the power or freedom to say no, but is in fact a slave to his lust. Galatians 5:19-21 describes the horrible consequences of these kinds of choices.

Instead, God wants men to pursue what is so much better. These verses in Galatians 5:22-25 describe a man who is defined by the Spirit; Philippians 4:8 describes a far more powerful man than one who is easily swayed by simple sin. We are called to be men who are true, noble and admirable. This kind of man is genuinely powerful!

CONSEQUENCES OF SEXUAL IMMORALITY

When a man gives in to the temptation of sex outside of marriage he opens himself to several destructive consequences:

1. **Physically.** He runs the risk of sexually transmitted diseases that can plague him the rest of his life. Literally millions of people are now living with the deadly results of STDs, HIV and AIDS. When a man has sex with a woman he makes himself vulnerable to the sexual history of every other person his partner has been with. Often that history is filled with disease.

He also toys with the possibility of pregnancy for his partner. He could be faced with enormous responsibilities and the demands of fatherhood far sooner than he's ready for them. Or he might face the profound moral battle of urging his partner to have an abortion.

2. *Emotionally.* The man who has premarital sex attaches himself to his partner. Our hearts are designed to bond with those we are intimate with, almost like Velcro. When that bond is broken, ignored and re-used repeatedly it results in emotional scars that keep a man from being able to fully bond with his future wife. He loses the ability to be vulnerable and faithful. He and his wife will both suffer as a result.

3. *Spiritually.* The immoral man finds himself increasingly distant from God. God forgives all those who sincerely confess their sin, but there are still undeniable consequences to sin. The man who chooses immorality is turning away from a deeper relationship with God and invites the emotions of remorse, guilt and shame into his life (I Corinthians 6:18).

Bible passages to read together:
> **Proverbs 23:27, 28** - Avoid promiscuous women
> **Jeremiah 2:12-13** - Do not dig broken wells that
>   can't hold water
> **I Corinthians 6:18-20; 9:24-27** - Run from sexual sin;
>   discipline yourself
> **I Thessalonians 4:3-8** - Avoid sexual immorality
> **Philippians 4:8** - Be noble, admirable men

Movie to watch together:
> *Lord of the Rings; Return of the King,* (Especially scene
>   70 The Crack of Doom.)

Discussion Questions

Dad:

1. What was your first exposure to pornography or sexual fantasies?

2. Do you have any regrets over choices you made in what you exposed yourself to?

3. What areas of sexual temptation do you struggle with today?

Son:

1. Have you been exposed to pornography? When did that first happen?

2. Do you experience sexual temptation at school? Do other kids brag about their experiences?

3. Would you like your dad's help in resisting temptation? How can he help you?

COVENANT OF COMMITMENT AND SUPPORT

We, _____ and _____,
covenant with each other to strive to create a clean heart around sexual
purity. We will elevate the status of women to a level of seeing them as
fearfully and wonderfully made by the Creator God, equal in status and
worth to ourselves.

We will strive to see sexuality as a wondrous and mysterious experience
between a man and a woman that completes the intimacy between them.
We will seek to look at women's eyes, and not their sexual areas, as a
practical way to focus on their worth.

We will work towards honesty with our struggles in this area, and will
confess difficulty and ask for help in prayer and encouragement. We do not
want to live in the shadows of deception in this area, because this will rob
us of strength and joy.

We will encourage one another to be Warriors in this area and to call upon
the strength of the True Warrior, Jesus, to build integrity in this great struggle.
We each invite the other to frequently check up on how we are doing with
this, not to shame, but to encourage each other, to invite openness with each
other so we remain committed in this journey of sexual purity.

_____
Dad's Signature

_____
Son's Signature

_____
Date

 ## II. HEART: The Compassion of a Lover

When men love God and others "with all of their heart" the quality that arises to the surface is Compassion. Compassion is not a characteristic that is usually considered manly. The way the word is commonly used may bring up images of softness or weakness for many men. But it is actually a very powerful quality; especially when strong men demonstrate it without a hint of embarrassment.

The word itself comes from a prefix (com), meaning "together or with," and a root word (passion) that means "suffering or pain." A man of compassion is a man who has the ability to get outside of his own concerns in order to connect deeply with the pain and feelings of others.

A man of compassion is aware of his own feelings; he is able to feel sad, afraid, angry, hurt, happy, or excited in situations that cause those kinds of emotions. He doesn't hide them or apologize for them. He is not ashamed of these feelings; on the contrary he knows that they allow him to be completely aware of what is going on in his life, and in the lives of others.

Often men are told as young boys that feelings are bad. Feelings of fear and sadness are often made fun of. "Don't be a baby," "Stop acting like a little girl," many boys are told when they cry or say they are afraid. This teaches boys to ignore or hide their feelings. As a result, boys and men have difficulty letting other males know that they actually have feelings, and so they hide them.

Those feelings don't just go away. They remain hidden and suppressed beneath the surface. Some day, they will return; and when they do, the reaction will be out of proportion to the trigger that causes them.

Picture a man raging at another driver who unintentionally swerves into his lane on a highway. His reaction is disproportionate to the incident that set him off. That's a clue that he has painful, and often unacknowledged, emotions just beneath the surface. Hidden, unexpressed emotions are like lava hidden from view, but very real and very powerful…waiting for the volcano to blow. Your dad probably knows what this feels like. Perhaps you do, too.

Compassionate men are connected with their heart and with the hearts of others

Emotions are given to us by God to help us be more aware of life and to experience it on the level of the heart. The natural order of things is to feel and to share these feelings with others in order to be understood, comforted, encouraged and helped. Because men often learn that they cannot share feelings without being judged, they often feel alone, sad or angry inside. They feel cut off from other people and do not always feel connected to what other people may be feeling.

Compassionate men are connected with their heart, and with the hearts of others. They share their feelings, in a constructive way, without fear or shame. Some feel a sense of trust and safety in sharing their own feelings in return. That's compassion.

Jesus was a man of compassion. He could cry, feel sadness, anger, loneliness, pity and even fear (picture him "sweating great drops of blood" in the Garden of Gethsemane) as he went about life. Because he was aware of his feelings, he was "moved with compassion" when he recognized similar feelings in others. This compassion allowed him to respond with comfort and concern to those who struggled.

Men who lack compassion are often insensitive to others. They can hurt people without conviction or concern. They have built a wall of indifference to the feelings of those around them. They have often walled off their own heart and can be completely unaware of how their behavior affects others. Compassion helps us live more wisely and sensitively.

The image of the man of compassion is that of the *Lover*. Lovers are often tuned in to the romantic, emotional aspects of life. Solomon was a lover. Read the Song of Solomon to discover the depth of feeling that he had. Artists and musicians often have a deep sense of feeling. They are able to sense the underlying beauty in a piece of art, a work of music or even in God's creation that surrounds us. Their gift is to express that beauty to the rest of us who may not even notice it.

Lovers courageously risk rejection by revealing themselves to others, and willingly make the cares and needs of people a priority in their lives. It's easy to stay distant; and it's easy to ignore the feelings and concerns of others. It takes effort and manly courage to deepen friendships and remain a faithful friend. Jesus was the greatest lover of all. Lovers are willing to follow his example.

Bible passages to read together:
> **Psalm 103:3-13** - God the Father is compassionate
> **2 Corinthians 1:3-7** - God is the Father of compassion
> **Ephesians 4:32-5:1** - Be compassionate to one another

Movie to watch together:
> *Shadowlands*

DISCUSSION QUESTIONS

Dad:

1. How did your father express his feelings? Was he open and honest about his sadness, loneliness, fears, hurts, etc.? Did he show compassion for you, as well as those around him?

2. Did you ever see your father cry? If so, what was it that caused him to? If not, why do you think that is?

Son:
1. Does your dad show his feelings to you? Do you know about his struggles in life, when he gets scared about things at work, or fears about being a good financial provider?

2. Does your dad ask you about your feelings? Do you feel safe to talk to him about your feelings? Have you ever let him see you cry? Why or why not?

NOTES

 ## ADMITTING AND HEALING WOUNDEDNESS

Men, and fathers in particular, have enormous influence in lives of others—for either blessing or destruction. Scripture foretold the powerful connection between fathers and children in the last verse in the Old Testament: "He will turn the hearts of the fathers to their children and the hearts of the children to their fathers; or else I will come and strike their land with a curse" Malachi 4:6.

That's how deeply important this relationship is. Many of us are, or will be, fathers; so these words speak directly to us. And every one of us is a descendent of a father. In other words, this prophecy is written to all of us, man or boy, father or son, mother or daughter. Our fathers have left an indelible impression on us—for blessing or for destruction.

In our society many fathers have not lived up to what their children needed; they have not passed on blessing. They didn't do so because their own fathers didn't. The impact of harmful fathers becomes a pattern passed on from generation to generation. In fact, the truth is, no father is perfect; every father passes on some wounds to his own children.

When God decided to build the family around fathers what did he have in mind for us? In Matthew 3:16, 17 we see a snapshot of what God gave his son. We see it again in Matthew 17:5 on the Mount of Transfiguration. He said:

"This is my son"

"I love him"

"I'm proud of him"

"Listen to him"

What do children need from their fathers? They need exactly what Jesus needed, and received:

1. *Acceptance (whole-hearted embrace).* A wise father demonstrates actions and speaks words that welcome who his son or daughter is by God's design. A son may feel a little embarrassed if his dad praises him in public. But deep inside he longs to know he is fully accepted by Dad.

2. *Affection (emotional as well as physical).* God the Father said, "This is my son; I love him." Children need to be told they are loved. They need to hear it and they need to feel it. Wise dads figure out age and gender-appropriate ways to touch, hug and even kiss their kids. Again, some of you boys reading this may deny any need to be told you are loved; but deep inside you were built by the Creator to hear those words by those who love you.

> ## Nothing can replace the words "I love you"

Nothing can replace the words "I love you" spoken to a son or a daughter by the father. Nothing. Those words communicate value and worth to any child. They pass on affection.

3. *Affirmation (telling him who he is).* God's words to Jesus demonstrated, "I am proud of him...just the way he is." These are words that build confidence in a child's identity and character. It's important that a father says, "I'm proud of you," *not* just when you for behave properly, but for *attributes* (dependability, creativity, compassion, generosity) that demonstrate strength of character.

4. *Anointing (who he can become).* Men need to be called out by their fathers and anointed. God the Father said, "Listen to him. He has something to say." It's been said that parents need to give

their children both Roots and Wings. Moms are so often intuitive protectors; they instill in their child a belief in their safety and in who they are. Moms establish roots. Dads are often encouragers; they instill in their child a belief in who they can become, what they bring to bear. Dads help develop wings in their kids.

These are the qualities children need to receive from their fathers: Acceptance, Affection, Affirmation and Anointing. Unfortunately, what children often receive from their fathers is quite different. Too often the hearts of fathers have turned away from their children. **As a result there is a curse; there is a wound:**

1. *Abandonment (physical distance).* In recent decades about 50 percent of marriages end in divorce; 75 percent of second marriages do as well. Usually that results in kids staying with their mothers during most of their childhood; meaning dads are away from their kids a majority of the years they are developing emotionally. By the time they are 18, 80 percent of American children will have spent time living apart from their father.

Many times this is not the father's preference, but for the kids the impact of a fatherless home remains. Sadly, sometimes this IS the choice of a father, who literally abandons his children.

What does that abandonment say to a boy? Dads, if you experienced this, what did it say to you? It says, "I don't want you." "You're not important to me. " This message passes on a deep wound of Abandonment to a child.

2. *Absence (physical presence, emotional absence).* Some dads remain present with their children, but are sleepwalking through the role. They spend most of their time consumed with work, financial concerns, tinkering in the garage or hanging out with their own friends. Some of us had dads like that.

What does that absence say to a boy? Dads, if you experienced this, what did it say to you? It says, "You're not worth my time." "I don't care about you." This message passes on a deep wound of Absence to a child.

3. Abuse (physical, verbal, spiritual or emotional damage). Some fathers unleash their own pain onto their kids. They haven't owned up to their own anger, emptiness or woundedness, and so they lash out at those closest to them.

In exactly the same way God designed us with heart, soul, mind and strength, those are the same ways sons (and daughters) can be deeply wounded:
- Heart—words that damage a son's freedom to feel and express emotions.
- Soul—words or actions that damage a boy's ability to believe that God loves him.
- Mind—harmful, shaming words that attack a son's intellectual ability.
- Strength—physical abuse that breaks, cuts or harms a boy's body and spirit.

What do these kinds of abuse say to a boy? Dads, if you experienced them (and we all did to some degree), what did they say to you? The messages passed on by these kinds of behavior are, "You're defective." "You're bad." "You're worthless." "I hate you." These are enormous wounds of abuse that may take a lifetime to heal.

What are the consequences of having a father like this? Exodus 20:5 tells us that the sins of the father are passed on to their children for three and four generations. The destructive inheritance a man receives becomes the damaged legacy he passes on. It is that simple, and that sad. Unless we admit our own woundedness and pursue healing and change, men will automatically pass on to our kids the same thing we received. Then they will do the same.

In a worst case, a boy grows up believing the message that he's not worth his father's presence, that he's not worth his father's time, or that he's simply worthless. These are the deepest possible wounds because they pierce the heart of a man's identity.

Many boys grow up with a vague doubt as to whether they have what it takes to be a real man. Many conclude that they need to:
- work harder in life to please their fathers
- prove their fathers wrong by doing better at some goal than them
- measure up to what they suspect their fathers really wanted in them: successful businessmen, star athletes or spiritual giants

All of these messages go directly to a boy's identity, and then they become the man's. They are what has been called the "Father Wound." All men have one. And they leave a deep scar.

What do those scars look like? They look like:

1. Anger. This is the Aggressive Man who is committed to protecting himself from further hurt by controlling others and circumstances. His inner anger hides (in fact, it reveals) a man's inner insecurity. It reveals his belief that he may not have what it takes to measure up as a man, and so he becomes driven to succeed in the eyes of those who matter most to him. Angry men respond in control, performance, intimidation and isolation.

2. Fear. This is the Passive Man who is committed to protecting himself by withdrawing to avoid yet another conflict or failure. He will pull away from others in order to avoid another reminder that he may not really measure up.

Have you ever had an experience where, in most relationships you feel comfortable and relatively at ease, but there's this one person, who, when he confronts you in the classroom or comes to your workplace, when he asks a question, when he offers unsolicited advice, you respond in insecurity and fear?

It's like a different "you" pops to the surface whenever he speaks to you. He touches your wound, and fear crawls to the surface. Fearful men respond with passivity and isolation.

3. Shame. We've already mentioned the profound depth of shame in men's lives. A father's voice and presence is the first imprint from an "outsider" for a child. The father is often the first adult in a child's life, outside of his mother, who has been physically and emotionally present with the child from before he was born, and in every aware moment of his life.

The love and presence of the father demonstrates to a son (or daughter) that he has intrinsic worth and value. Absence, abandonment or abuse from a father bestows deep shame.

The Father Wound is the difference between what you received from your earthly father and what God the Father designed you to long for and need. Because no human father is perfect, every son has this wound. Every son. But there is healing from this wound.

How do we heal from a Father Wound?

1. *We acknowledge we are wounded.* The first step to healing is in the quiet depths of our hearts. Healing resides in facing not only the wounds we have received, but in the dark lies that we have heard from others and believed about ourselves; they are the agreements we have made with the author of lies, Satan. Lies such as, "You'll never amount to anything," "You must be better than everyone else," "I'm ashamed of you," "You should be ashamed of yourself," and "You're not fit to be a man."

The miracle of God's grace in our lives is that he not only will heal our wound, he uses it to draw us to himself. The man who can clearly see what his earthly dad did not, or could not, give him will be more likely to ask God for it.

What's more, God redeems our wounds and turns them into sources of transformation and passion.

2. *We grieve our wounds.* Ignoring our wound, pretending that it doesn't exist, only prolongs its effect. We need to have the courage and honesty to admit, yes, our fathers (or our mothers, churches, coaches, teachers or society) were not all we needed them to be.

Some were very good, but even they had wounds they passed on to us. There is a painful gap between what they were able to give us, and what God has in mind for us. That realization may bring grief and sadness to our hearts. It should never bring shame and blame.

3. *We take the step of forgiveness.* Wallowing in grief, anger or sadness does no one any good. Having acknowledged the fact that we are wounded men, and boys, having felt the sadness of living in a broken world, and having accepted the fact that short-term relief doesn't heal the wound, we can move on to genuine healing.

The road to healing goes through forgiveness. In his book *The Bondage Breaker*, Neil Anderson says, "The residue of anger, bitterness, is the acid that eats its own container." By hanging on to blame and vengefulness we think we are keeping those who wounded us on the hook. The fact is we are keeping ourselves on the hook.

In Colossians 3:12 and 13 we are urged:

> Therefore, as God's chosen people, holy and dearly loved, clothe yourselves with compassion, kindness, humility, gentleness and patience. Bear with each other and forgive whatever grievances you may have against one another. Forgive as the Lord forgave you.

Dads and sons, as you read this, God may be bringing feelings to the surface that you have rarely felt before. Do not deny them or retreat from them. Be courageous. Acknowledge and embrace them. They're your wounds and they are sacred.

God is a God of healing. He has power over the Enemy and the consequences of any harmful wounds we receive from the hands of others. Psalm 30: 2 says, "Lord, my God, I called to you for help, and you healed me." Psalm 147:3 promises that "He heals the brokenhearted and binds up their wounds." When healed, our wounds can be redeemed. They become the source of a new level of tenderness, compassion, conviction and passion that you may never have known before. That's why wounds are sacred.

Bible passages to read together:
Isaiah 57:18, 19 - I will heal them
Jeremiah 17:14; 33:6 - God heals his people
Acts 3:16 - Jesus gives complete healing
James 5:16 - Pray for healing
Any Gospel There are 92 references to Jesus healing the wounded or sick

Movie to watch together:
The Kid

DISCUSSION QUESTIONS

Dad:
1. Can you relate to any of the wounds or scars listed above? Which ones? Where do you think they came from?

2. Have you ever heard of the concept of a Father Wound before? If it's true that your father has passed on a significant wound to you (and it is), which do you think are yours?

3. When have you ever taken time to acknowledge, grieve and forgive that wound? If you haven't, your son needs you to; are you willing to do that? When and how will you?

4. The Bible says that the sins of the father are laid in the laps of his children. Which hurtful sins, or even destructive family patterns, do you think you have passed on to your son? Have you apologized to him for those? If not, will you? When?

Son:
1. Have you felt any abandonment, absence or abuse from your dad? What would it take for you to let him know, or ask someone else's help to let him know, how much it hurts?

2. Do you notice any sin patterns or harmful family traits that you keep practicing? What are they? Would you be willing to pray from healing for those patterns? Would you be willing to ask someone else to pray for you? Who? When?

3. Have you told your dad you forgive him? If not, do you think you can do that? When?

NOTES

 # Family Story Exercise

(Used at retreats with Craig or another guide.)

Together you and your son are to research your family story on both your side of the family and your wife's, or if you're unmarried, your son's mother.

Go back at least three generations from your son, to at least your grandparents and his mother's. If you can go back further please do it. Contact any family members by phone, email or letter, or research online to find out as much information about your son's ancestors as possible. This will take time, so please plan ahead.

Your son should be the primary interviewer as well as presenter of the info to our group, but you may need to keep the fire lit under him to make the contacts and get the assignment done by the retreat.

Primary information to be sure to include, to the extent you can uncover it:
- names, birth dates and dates of death
- location of birth and death
- occupations

KEY ASSIGNMENT:
- Record all **positive traits** and characteristics (hard-working, Christian, integrity, good father, dependable, provider, spiritual leader) for each ancestor, especially men.
- Record all **harmful traits** (angry, abusive, alcoholic, imprisoned, divorced, no spiritual faith, promiscuity, lust) for each ancestor, especially men.

At the retreat you will transfer your discoveries onto a poster board provided to you, so others can see and follow your son's story as he walks us through it. You will record positive traits in blue; harmful traits in red. Remember, the son will be the presenter.

Following each father/son story will be one of the most significant moments of the retreat, and of the Passage experience. We will ask your son to point out any harmful patterns that your family has historically passed on. Then we will ask you if you have also passed on that same pattern, or any other that you may regret.

We won't force you, but we will respectfully ask you, if you want to say anything to your son about that. ***Your full ownership and apology for that pattern can be one of the most powerful, meaningful and liberating things you can ever do for your son.*** (Think how much you wish your dad had done this for you.)

A genuine apology has these components:
- You admit what you did. Be specific. "When I lost my temper I hit you."
- You admit the consequences. "I know this caused you to lose trust in me."
- You take sole ownership. "It was wrong of me. I'm so sorry."
- You never include the word "but," making excuses or shifting of blame.

After that we will pray a blessing over your son; that he will live out the positive qualities in his story—and the harmful ones will end with him. Men, don't miss this opportunity. Stay on track on the assignment and bring your heart to whatever you say. If you get emotional, you won't be the only one. And you will *never, ever* regret it.

NOTES

 # HONORING WOMEN

I deally, men grow up with healthy experiences with the women in their lives. If they had mothers who were loving and responsive to their needs, boys develop a deep sense of love and appreciation for the sacrificial care their mothers showed them. If they observed their fathers honoring their mothers and treating them with a deep sense of respect, they got the message that mothers and females in general are honorable and deserve respectful treatment.

On the other hand, if a boy sees his father treat women with a demeaning, condescending or fearful attitude, he is likely to take on that same approach to women. That son receives a poor role model and negative views about mothers and, therefore, women in general. Just like wounds, these patterns are often passed down through family generations.

One way that some men keep women in an inferior position is to treat them only as sexual objects to be played with. Men who do this reduce women to a "piece of meat," valuable only for the pleasure of men. Our society communicates this message by demeaning portrayals of women on TV, in magazines, in music, in movies. These destructive messages are most explicitly communicated in virtually all pornography.

If a mother is able to allow her son a developing sense of freedom and responsibility as he grows older, the adult son is able to establish his identity apart from her without conflict, while maintaining a relationship that affirms her significance as a source of counsel and comfort. The son does not devalue the mother, but instead, lifts her up and honors her.

On the other hand, if a boy's mother abuses him, or coddles him unnecessarily, refusing to allow him to go on the masculine journey with her blessing, that son will likely develop feelings of self-doubt and animosity toward his mother, and then other women in his life. *In this way mothers play a deeply profound role in the healthy masculine development of their sons.*

Moms often focus on nurture and concern for a child's security. Dads are often the encouragers of accomplishment and development. The two influences are both valuable and necessary and of equal importance. God always wanted these differences to be complementary, and never competitive.

God created both men and women in his image (Genesis 1:26, 27); both have intrinsic (basic) worth and value. Although men and women are uniquely different in their bodies, and in some emotional and relational characteristics, they do not differ in their worth. Gender differences are part of God's wonderfully creative pattern of meeting the complex needs of people.

Men are often, though not always, more aggressive physically, task-oriented, and accomplishment-driven than women. This appears to have been useful in men's early roles of providers in a more hunting or farm-based economy. It took a good deal of physical skill and tolerance to capture animals, or plow fields, for food. Historically, these qualities motivated men to be the primary providers for families by developing work, a trade and eventually working outside of the home.

Women are often, though not always, more attuned to the senses, emotions and are more relationship-oriented than most men; this is of great value in building deep, authentic connections with others. Males tend to be a bit more prone to taking risks and developing new physical skills, while females tend to be more tuned in to intuitive discernment and sensitivity to relationship issues.

> Women play a deeply profound role in the healthy masculine development of their sons

Of course, not all men, nor all women, are exactly alike. Some men are exceptionally relational; some women are exceptionally goal-oriented. But by and large, men and women demonstrate the tendencies mentioned above. The exceptions are just that—exceptional.

A healthy man learns how to blend his own aspects of the tenderness of the female with the aggressiveness of the male. Men who cannot learn from women tend to be intimidating, overly aggressive and insensitive. This is often due to a fear of women and a distorted assumption that women are out to change or control men. Men in this position are not able to grow and adapt and often end up in isolation and loneliness.

By God's design, both men and women long for two deep needs to be fulfilled: To be *loved*, and to be *respected*. By and large, men long more to be respected, women long more to be loved. As a result, a man's greatest desire is to accomplish tasks that bring respect; his greatest fear as a result is *failure*, the loss of respect from others. A woman's greatest desire is to be pursued, known and loved; her greatest fear as a result is *abandonment*, the loss of intimacy and relationship.

Interestingly, the Bible implies the same. Ephesians 5 tells both husbands and wives to submit to one another (5:21) and then goes on to tell wives to submit, or give respect to, their husbands (5:22), exactly what they long for most. Men are told to love their wives (5:25); give them exactly what they long for most. In both cases, it's also exactly what we find hardest to give each other. Women struggle to submit well; men struggle to love well. It's no wonder marriage can be so hard!

Once again it needs to be said, these descriptions are not exclusively male and female. All men and women demonstrate some blend of these traits. But, in general, these are the tendencies we see reflected in men and women. Both of these tendencies, the longing for love and the longing for respect, are valuable because they reflect the nature of God.

The differences between men and women are most obvious in our physical design. God created sexuality as a model of the different, though complementary, nature of relationships. The very design of our most characteristic physical parts, our reproductive organs, reflects the design of our "hearts" our God-given nature.

Physically men extend; when aroused, they point, they lead. As John Eldredge says, they "rise to the occasion"; they move toward their wives. They penetrate the deepest parts of her body and her soul, with firmness and great tenderness (Richard Rohr's insightful analogy). They empty themselves to bring about new life.

Physically females are open. They are receptive but usually need a higher level of relationship and trust to respond openly. When they do, they entrust, they receive and surround their husband, providing protection and comfort. In doing so, they bring about life itself.

In healthy, God-honoring sexual relations, the male must be sensitive to the needs of the female for trust and safety in order for her to be receptive. This is also true for relational intimacy.

In Christ there is no distinction in value between male and female

To be honoring to women, men must appreciate the unique differences that women possess and be willing to see these differences as valuable and equal to men's. Men and women, who honor these innate differences, seek to learn from each other, rather than demean each other, and commit to respect each other and rely upon one another's strengths.

In any case, never forget, women are of equal value as men. In Christ, there is no distinction in value between male and female. Each is equally a reflection of God's character, equally valued and accepted by Christ, and they share equally in being children of the Father and heirs to all that God provides for his children (Galatians 3:28).

Men should never aggressively intimidate women into submission to their needs, but instead, we should take initiative by demonstrating love the way Jesus did—through self-sacrifice. We'll say it again, in no way are male/female distinctives connected to intrinsic worth. Men are not greater or lesser in value to women; nor are women to men. By God's design, we are simply different. Wonderfully—often frustratingly—different.

Bible passages to read together:
 Genesis 1:26, 27 - Women are made in God's image
 Genesis 3:1-19 - Like man, woman sinned and was cursed in profoundly deep places (her longing for men, and her ability to give birth)
 Ephesians 5:21-28 - Submit to one another; love your wife like Christ does

Movie to watch together:
 Spiderman 2 (Especially scenes 50 and 51)

DISCUSSION QUESTIONS

Dad:
1. What did you observe in your father's relationship to your mother or other females and how has that influenced your view of females?

2. Share with your son your experience with your mother and other significant women in your life and how that has influenced the way that you see females. Do you feel that you have a positive or negative view of women and their differences from you? How have you handled this?

Son:
1. In what ways does your father talk about or treat women? How has your dad's behavior toward your mother influenced your feelings about women?

2. What have your experiences been with your mother or other significant women in your life? Has this left you with a positive or negative attitude towards women? Do you feel angry towards women?

Dad and Son:

1. Read Genesis 3:1-19 and discuss the actions and attitudes demonstrated by Adam and by Eve in this story. How do you see these same attitudes between men and women continued today?

2. Discuss the honorable characteristics of women and commit to elevating their status in your eyes and behavior. Affirm their worth by expressing your appreciation in practical ways to your wife/mother.

Make a commitment to look at women with respect and not with lust. Lust diminishes and dehumanizes women. Respect elevates them. Look at the eyes of women and not at sexual parts. This reflects a desire to express the essential God-created worth that women have.

NOTES

 ## III. MIND: The Conviction of a Mentor

When men love God and others with all their Mind, that is, with all of their intellect, they live as men of Conviction. They know what principles they believe in. They have a clear sense of what is right and what is wrong. When they are faced with temptation or when they see others behave in ways that break a moral code, they are willing to stand up and say, "I disagree with that; I won't do it."

Men of conviction are not afraid to boldly state what they believe, even when it is not popular. They do not do things just to get accepted by others, whether at work or at school. They do what they believe is honoring to God.

Men of conviction are not wishy-washy about their values and convictions. They seek truth and when they find it they use that truth as the guiding principle by which they live their lives.

Men of conviction rely on God's Word as the foundation of their beliefs

Men of conviction rely on God's Word as the foundation of their beliefs. They see the Bible as a sword that cuts error away from truth. Hebrews 4:12 says, "The Word of God is living and active. Sharper than any double-edged sword, it penetrates even to dividing soul and spirit, joints and marrow; judges the thoughts and attitudes of the heart." Men of conviction use the Bible to help them determine what kind of men they really want to be.

The image that describes men of conviction is the *Mentor*. Mentors are wise men who pass on their experience and wisdom to others who are usually younger and less experienced in life. They are far more concerned with deep wisdom than superficial information. I Corinthians 8:1 tells us "knowledge puffs up." In other words simply gaining lots of information about things tends to make men proud.

Far better is the pursuit of wisdom. Books like Proverbs literally plead with the reader to "seek wisdom, pursue wisdom, chase after wisdom," at all costs. Wisdom is clearly the distinguishing factor between a man who lives his life foolishly and the man whose life is admirable. Dads, sons, pay attention to this! It is truly one of the most important principles in life.

Mentors have learned not to rely solely on their own judgment because they know that it is flawed and easily confused by their tendency to be self-centered. They admit their own weaknesses and limitations, so they themselves have listened to older men who made wise choices and are now living truly joyful, fulfilled lives. In turn, mentors pass on that same wisdom to the next generation.

Consistent with God's Word, they have learned to value people and relationships rather than solely accomplishment and fame. They follow after Paul's counsel to pursue "whatever is true, whatever is noble, whatever is right, whatever is pure, whatever is lovely, whatever is admirable..." (Philippians 4:8).

Jesus was a man of conviction. He knew who he was, what his principles were, and what his purpose in life was. He had come to do the will of his Father. He had come to "seek and to save that which is lost." When he was challenged or accused of wrong, he did not waver, because he was convinced that he was following the truth.

Jesus' calling was so clear to him that he said; "I know where I came from and where I am going…my decisions are right because I am not alone. I stand with the Father who sent me" (John 8:14, 16). He is the model for healthy men of conviction.

Jesus, as well, is the best example we can find of a mentor. He not only spoke to crowds in the thousands, passing on to them teaching like they had never heard before, but he confronted the pious teachers of religious law by exposing their hypocrisy. He gathered around him a group of close followers who he poured his life into. That handful of men went on to form the Church and literally influence the whole world.

In all these ways Jesus demonstrated deep wisdom and a deep commitment to stand by his convictions no matter the cost. In the end it cost him his life. But in giving up his life, he changed history.

Bible passages to read together:
> **Proverbs 1:1-7; 20-22** - Wisdom brings understanding; wisdom calls to us
> **Proverbs 2** - Benefits of wisdom
> **Proverbs 3:13-26** - Benefits of wisdom
> **Proverbs 4:4-9** - Wisdom is supreme

Movies to watch together:
> *Dead Poets Society* (Especially scenes 3 and 4)
> *The Horse Whisperer* (Especially scene 20)
> *Finding Forrester*

DISCUSSION QUESTIONS

Dad:

1. Did your dad teach you what to value and how to act? What values did you learn by listening to your dad and watching his life? Did he value money, power, position, winning, or accomplishment? Or did he value people and relationships? How has this affected your life?

2. Who do you view as being a mentor in your life when you were younger? What wisdom did he pass on to you?

3. Who is a mentor in your life now? If you don't have one, why not? Who is a man you might ask to become your mentor? Are you mentoring a younger man?

Son:

1. What is your dad teaching you about life and what is most important? What do you think are the most important principles in his life?

2. Do you feel free to go to your dad to ask questions to help you deal with decisions you have to make in your life? Have you let him know that you'd like to have those kinds of conversations?

3. Is there an older student at school or church you could imagine inviting to be a mentor to you? What would it take for you to ask him?

N O T E S

 # BUILDING CHARACTER: The Fruit of the Spirit

(Author's note: I'm indebted to Lew Caliento, a friend and mentor, for much of the content in the following section.)

"Character," a wise person once said, "is who we are when no one is looking." The hobbies men choose reveal *what we enjoy*; the occupations men choose reveal *what we do*; our character reveals *who we are*. Character defines us.

For many people, being a person of good character isn't really that important. People will work at being happy, wealthy, thin or even tan. But working on character? Who cares? A lot of people don't even think that character matters in leadership. This is a major issue facing our nation right now because of some political, business and church leaders' unethical or immoral behavior.

As followers of Christ we are called to overcome our sinful nature and to serve one another in love. Yet, we find ourselves constantly struggling with our sinful nature. We seem to be continuously called to make decisions that test the nature of our character.

Even the Apostle Paul struggled with his sinful nature. In Romans 7:15 he wrote, "I do not understand what I do. For what I want to do, I don't do, but what I hate, I do." This is the battle that virtually all Christian men can identify with, desiring strong character in our lives yet continuing to struggle with lingering elements of sin.

In this battle it is extremely important to keep a couple of things in mind:
- There is NO condemnation for those who are in Christ Jesus (Romans 8:1). We renounce any attempts of the Enemy to cast shame over us due to failure.
- We continue to press on toward the goal of Christ-like character. Paul said, " But one thing I do: Forgetting what is behind and straining toward what is ahead, I press on toward the goal to win the prize for which God has called me heavenward in Christ Jesus" (Philippians 3:13, 14).

What does it take to build character? We need to long for and pray for the Fruit of the Spirit. We will find that to develop this fruit we need two things—faith in Jesus Christ and the commitment to allow our lives to be increasingly controlled by the Holy Spirit.

In Galatians 5:22, 23, the Fruit of the Spirit provides a wonderful description of what character consists of:

Love: the kind of unconditional love for others that God has.

Joy: deep fulfillment and peace regardless of our circumstances.

Peace: a lasting sense of contentment based on the fact that God is in charge.

Patience: the ability to let go of the demand that other people do what we want.

Kindness: demonstrating consideration and compassion toward others.

Goodness: knowing and doing God's will.

Faithfulness: being dependable; doing what you say you will do.

Gentleness: a secure strength of personality that doesn't need to flaunt its power.

Self-control: the ability to draw the line on harmful desires.

Here are some practical guides to help you become a man whose life is based on a foundation of rock-solid character:

Find role models, mentors. We need to find models of good character. In the Bible, read about choices made by wise men like Moses, Daniel, Joseph, Joshua, John the Baptist, Peter, Paul, and most important, Jesus. Read articles or biographies about present-day men who stand their ground in the face of pressure.

When you are facing pressure to conform to someone else's standards, Stop and Think. Ask yourself, "Is the way I'm acting the way I'd want to be treated?" Or, ask yourself, "If everybody else does what I'm about to do, would the world be a better or worse place?" Or, "Is this the way Jesus would act if he were in my position?"

Determine your direction. Most of what we do, good or bad, we do out of habit. The first time you cheat, or are honest, it's difficult. The tenth time it's easy. Both good and evil become habits. God has made it your choice. What direction do you want your life to go? Each decision you make will affect that direction—even if no one else knows about it!

Live it. Be aware of how you are acting. Remember, God gave us the freedom to choose right or wrong, love or selfishness, genuine strength or weakness. Which choices are you going to make day by day?

Someone has wisely said, "Sow (plant) a thought, reap an action; sow an action, reap a habit; sow a habit, reap a lifestyle; sow a lifestyle, reap a destiny." Every action, large or small, defines who we will become as men. These actions form our destiny and our legacy.

Bible passages to read together:
  Daniel 3 - Men of enormous conviction
  John 18 – Jesus' courage and character in the face of threats and death
  Acts 4:5-21 - Peter and John stand their ground
  Romans 7:14-8:6 - The battle between the sinful nature and the life of the Spirit
  Galatians 5:13-26 - Fruit of the Spirit

Movie to watch together:
  3:10 to Yuma (Especially scene 20)

DISCUSSION QUESTIONS

Dad and Son:

1. Do you understand why the Fruit of the Spirit is important? Why is it so hard to attain?

2. Who do you know from work or school or among your friends or relatives who most exemplifies the Fruit of the Spirit? Why? What do you see in them that you admire?

3. Taking turns, go through each Fruit of the Spirit and answer the question: "Do you see this fruit in me?" Help each other. If a particular fruit is missing or could be stronger, tell each other.

4. Think of a particular aspect of the Fruit of the Spirit that you feel you most need to develop. What is one step you can take to develop that aspect?

Pray together. Ask God to help you exercise and develop the Fruit of the Spirit. Pray that God will make you men of rock-solid, Spirit-powered character.

NOTES

 # BUILDING A BAND OF BROTHERS

(Author's note: I'm grateful to Vance Brown, a friend and brother, for his contribution to this section.)

H ave you ever been on a great team? Perhaps you were on an academic team in elementary school; or a sports team in middle school; or a music team in high school. What is it about being on a team that makes it so enjoyable? Most people would say that teams have some of the following characteristics. A team:
- has a clear purpose to accomplish
- is made up of a variety of people; not everyone is the same
- does things that only one person by himself can't
- consists of members who believe in and trust each other
- adds excitement, fun, or accomplishment to life
- is greater than the sum of its parts

A lot of men can look back at certain periods of their lives and identify a team they were a part of. Frequently those are some of the best memories of their lives.

Sadly, many of those men have never experienced the trust, the companionship and the support of those relationships ever since. Sure they may have a work team at the office, or they may be part of a weekly bowling team. But when it comes to really having deep, trusting friendships with other men, most men live in isolation, living lives of "quiet desperation," as Henry David Thoreau put it.

Why do you suppose that is? A big part of the answer is due to the "image" versus the "reality" of being a man.

Our culture is filled with powerful communication forms known as the "media." The media in America consists of what we see on TV, the Internet, in movies, what we hear in music and what we read in books or magazines. What images do the media portray that men should be like? It's pretty obvious that beer commercials, sports shoe ads, magazine covers, cop shows and war movies have fairly similar messages:
- if you want it, take it
- crush your competition
- don't trust anyone, you're on your own
- winning is the ultimate goal
- your desires are more important than others' are
- Just Do It!

The underlying message to men is that everyone else, especially other men, is your competition. Do whatever it takes to beat them and get what you want.

That's the image. The reality? If you get men to honestly reveal what goes through their mind at work, how they feel when competing with other guys, or what keeps them awake during the middle of the night, you'd hear a very different message.

The truth is more like:
- I'm not sure I have what it takes to be a man.
- I'm scared to death I'm going to screw up.
- If people really knew me they'd want nothing to do with me.
- I feel stuck in a role without meaning.
- I'm alone—and I'm angry!

It's not a pretty picture, is it? The commitment to hide these emotions from others leads to even greater isolation. It's been said, "A man in isolation is one decision away from disaster." Without friends or input, in the darkness of secrecy, a man can make an awful decision in an instant that will haunt him the rest of his life. That isolation magnifies the lie that says, " I'm the only guy like me. I've got to hide the real me from everyone else." And so on goes a destructive cycle that propels itself.

"A man in isolation is known by his weaknesses; a man in community is known by his strengths." When a man keeps his secret sins to himself, the lies and accusations from the Devil remind himself that he is broken, flawed, hopelessly defective, unworthy of being loved and accepted. All of those are lies of shame.

It's when a man opens his life to others and shares his vulnerabilities and mistakes with other men, the hidden power over those sins is broken, he receives acceptance from his friends, he is known and loved more deeply. Most important, he knows he is forgiven and accepted by God (I John 1:7).

"I'm the only guy like me."
Nothing could be further from the truth. The fact is that most men encounter messages of doubt like these. Keeping them secret gives them greater power.

Proverbs 27:17 says, "As iron sharpens iron, so one man sharpens another." One man's input and insight can be God's tool to bring about sharpening, strength and power to another man. Dads and sons, it's a very wise man who makes a priority of surrounding himself with a few trusted men that he invites into the deeper levels of his life.

The TV miniseries *Band of Brothers* is the story of a special unit, Easy Company of the 101st Airborne Division in World War II. They were dropped behind enemy lines on D-Day and fought some of the bloodiest battles of the war—from the beaches of Normandy, through the Battle of the Bulge, all the way to the fall of Adolf Hitler's Eagle's Nest war headquarters. These were men committed to fighting for each other, trusting one another, defending any man who is under attack, breaking the power of evil and injustice.

Men, we need to be a part of a Band of Brothers with men like that. But our Enemy today is not just a mad man like Hitler. Ephesians 6:12 tells us, "For our struggle is not against flesh and blood, but against the rulers, against the authorities, against the powers of this dark world and against the spiritual forces of evil in the heavenly realms."

Men matter, they just don't think so

The greatest battles men face are of a spiritual nature: we doubt that we matter; we succumb to pleasure-seeking, soul-killing behavior; we believe the lies of Shame that the Enemy whispers in our ears; we avoid meaningful connection with others on a spiritual level. The solution to those battles is to never try to fight them alone. The solution is to bring other men into our life.

What are the benefits of befriending like-minded men? That kind of community brings:
- honesty
- trust
- safety
- loyalty
- effectiveness
- encouragement
- growth
- transformation
- joy

Dads, do you have a Band of Brothers you trust and commit yourself to? Sons, what would it take to start friendships like this with a few other guys? It would take:
- **Confidence:** rejecting embarrassment over who you are, being convinced God designed you *on* purpose and *for a* purpose.
- **Conviction:** believing that the kind of men we surround ourselves with affects the kind of man we become.
- **Compassion:** being willing to care about the lives of other men and letting them into our own.
- **Courage:** taking action in the face of fear in order to make something happen.

In short, it takes manliness. You both can do it. If you do, your Band of Brothers can become the greatest, most significant team experience of your life.

Bible passages to read together:
   I Samuel 20 - The brotherhood of David and Jonathan
   Proverbs 18:24 - A friend sticks closer than a brother
   Ephesians 6:10-18 - Our battle is spiritual
   Hebrews 10:24, 25 - Cheer one another on
   I John 1:7 - Walk openly with other men

Movies to watch together:
   Saving Private Ryan (Especially scene 14)
   Band of Brothers (Miniseries)
   The Guardian (Especially scene 11)

DISCUSSION QUESTIONS

Dad:
1. What was the best team you were ever a part of? What was the worst team you were ever on? What was the difference?

2. Can you relate to the description above of the questions men are really asking of themselves? Which ones in particular? Do you have any friends you tell that to? If so, when did you make that decision? If not, what has kept you from finding some men that you can trust?

Son:
1. Does this idea make sense to you? Do you understand why it's important to invite a team of close fiends into your life? What part of it doesn't make sense?

2. Are there two or three other guys you could ask to have this kind of friendship with you? Who are they? How would you ask them? What would be the hardest part? How could you overcome that challenge?

Dad and Son:
What commitment do you want to make with each other about being able to talk honestly about the issues men struggle with?

 ## IV. SOUL: The Confidence of a King

Men who are confident have a deep internal sense that they are valuable. They have what we call "good self-esteem." What this means is that they know that they are loved and accepted for *who they are*, not just *what they do*. They don't think they are better than other people, nor do they believe that they are less than other people. They have a confident assurance that their lives are as important as anyone else's. Yet no more important.

The unique basis of this confidence and assurance of worth for followers of Jesus is the fact that the very Creator of the universe created us on purpose and for a purpose. God loves us. He demonstrated this love by sending his son to die on a cross to restore us to a place of great honor—we are his heirs, his sons.

This is the foundation of our confidence. That the One who created us says that we have worth and majesty. The True Father has lifted us up to a place of great honor.

The image of what deep inner confidence looks like is that of the *King*. Kings in olden times had ultimate authority and power over those they ruled. That was without question. However, kings showed a great difference in how they used their power. Some, like Saul and Nebuchadnezzar in the Bible, used their authority to dominate and control others. Both of these men even went so far as to kill those who threatened them.

Ironically, this violent use of their power revealed a deep inner weakness—they had no confidence in their ability to lead, or in the willingness of their subjects to freely follow them. Their lack of confidence resulted in fear, insecurity and, ultimately, the violent control of others.

King David, on the other hand, although he also had serious failures, demonstrated the confidence of a king who has the authority of God's blessing. He was described as "a man after [who pursued] God's own heart." Because David tried to honor God with his power he had the confidence of God's blessing. God lifts up, or strengthens, men who want to honor him and who truly want to use their strength to help others, rather than to protect their position.

Read the story of the Prodigal Son in Luke 15. The father in that story is a picture of God the Father. The son is a symbol of all of us as lost children. Notice how the father lifts up the son and restores him to a place of high prominence and value. This is a picture of how God lifts up men to a place of high esteem as his sons. In fact, the Bible says that we can call him Dad (*Abba*), the affectionate term for a loving and caring father. We are lifted up in his arms and this deep inner sense of our worth to God is the basis of a true sense of confidence.

Our human fathers can add to our confidence by lifting us up and recognizing our worth and value. Many men have experienced fathers who did not lift them up, but rather put them down either by criticizing and ridiculing them or by ignoring them. As I've pointed out earlier, many men carry around scars in their hearts that were created by deep longings for their father's love and acceptance. These unhealed men lack confidence because deep inside they feel as if they do not have value.

Good fathers model themselves after the Heavenly King. They love their sons unconditionally. They may not love the behavior of their sons and may discipline them to help them to grow, but they never cut off their love for the person. Good fathers regularly tell their sons that they love them.

> Confident men do not feel that they always have to compete with others to win approval

They are pleased with their sons much like the Father was pleased with his son, Jesus, when he said, "This is my son in whom I am well pleased" (Matthew 3:17). Words of affirmation and acceptance by a father create in a son a deep and abiding trust in his own worth and value. As we have seen in earlier lessons, men who have not had earthly fathers who have lifted them up can still experience healing and confidence by knowing the love of the True Father, God, our Heavenly King.

Healthy, confident men do not feel that they always have to compete with others in order to win approval. Rather, they are free to act with assurance that their performance is not going to change their inner value. They are men who demonstrate leadership because confidence inspires others to follow their lead. They are confident, but not cocky. They do not have a superior attitude toward others. In fact, they demonstrate humility that comes from confidence. In other words, they do not have to be right to prove their worth, and so they can admit to limitations.

Jesus is a model of supreme confidence. He knew who he was, what he believed in and what his mission was. He was able to handle criticism because he knew the truth.

There are two extremes of men who do not have inner confidence. One, the "tyrant man," looks strong on the outside because he comes on in a domineering fashion. This dominance, however, hides a deep fear of his own insignificance. He needs others to cower before him to somehow shore up his weak sense of confidence. He belittles and criticizes others to make them feel small and himself big and powerful. Confident men do not need the weakness of others to prove their strength.

The other extreme is the "passive man," who knows he has no confidence and feels he has nothing to offer. He has often been beaten into emotional submission by a tyrant father, and has no secure inner sense of worth. He feels weak because he has not measured up in the eyes of other men. He thinks he has not earned enough, been successful enough, or hurt others enough, to get the approval of other men.

The confident man knows that he has worth for who he is in a spiritual sense, the son of the Father. The King of the universe has called us his heirs, his sons. Through God, the godly man learns to demonstrate the true aspects of kingship and godly authority. This kind of man lives with that deep sense of inner reassurance. Men can experience this by building up a consistent, daily focus on who they are from God's point of view.

Bible passages to read together:
Psalm 139:13-16 - You are a special creation of God
John 3:16 - You are so loved and valued that God's son died for you
2 Corinthians 5:17 - You are a new creation of great worth
Romans 12:3 - Don't think of yourself as higher than others
Romans 8:14-17; Galatians 4:4-7 - We are God's sons and heirs
Ephesians 1:2 - You are blessed and have a heavenly status
James 4:10 - Be humble; God will elevate you

Movies to watch together:
First Knight (Especially scenes 17, 41 and 44)
Mr. Holland's Opus (Especially scenes 23 and 24)

DISCUSSION QUESTIONS

Dad:

1. Are you confident of your own worth and value, or do you struggle to know that you have great significance?

2. What influences you to conclude whether you have value or not? Do you tend to place your value on your income, possessions or your work?

3. How did your dad lift you up and let you know that no matter what you did, he still loved you? Did you ever feel that you were not good enough, or never got recognized just for who you are?

Son:

1.When do you feel valued by your dad? Are there certain things you do that you know your dad appreciates?

2. Do you ever feel that you have to somehow measure up to his standards to be accepted or for him to be proud of you? How do you feel about this?

3. If you feel angry about not being accepted, let your dad know this so he can understand how his approach affects you.

   (Dad, be sure to honor your son's courage in being honest with you! Let him know his feelings are safe with you.)

NOTES

 # GOD RULES!

Some people don't believe God exists (they are called atheists) or they might say they just aren't certain whether he does or not (agnostic). The vast majority, however, consistently indicate in national surveys that they do believe in God.

Unfortunately, many of these people don't view God as being an important part of their lives. They live as if he doesn't exist. (Author Parker Palmer calls these folks Functional Atheists. "Those who talk a good game about God," but live as if he doesn't really matter.)

A man of God bases his whole life on the fact that God exists and he is sovereign—he is his king.

HOW DO WE KNOW FOR SURE THERE IS A GOD?

It is pretty hard to prove, otherwise there wouldn't be any dis-agreement about it. Many wise thinkers and religious scholars have come up with dozens of arguments for his existence; some of them are quite complicated. No single argument gives complete proof. But taken as a whole, they are convincing. Let's look at a few.

1. **The universal idea of God.** The study of almost all human cul-tures shows that a consistent conviction of people throughout history is a belief in God. From the most primitive tribes to the most advanced societies, the idea of a supreme being has been a common belief.

Ecclesiastes 3:11 says that God has "set eternity in the hearts of man." Blaise Pascal, the 17th century mathematician, described this as "the God-shaped vacuum" in the hearts of all men and women. All mankind has a spiritual hunger that must be filled.

2. **The amazing complexity of the universe.** What do you sup-pose would be the chances of a tornado blowing through a junkyard and accidentally forming a 747? Infinitesimally small! That's about the chance of a universe like ours, with human bod-ies as complex as ours, just happening by random coincidence.

> **All mankind has a spiritual hunger that must be filled**

One mathematician determined that the time it would take for a person to solve a Rubik's Cube puzzle, one step each second, blindfolded would be 13.5 trillion years. The ran-dom formation of the building blocks of living cells would take even longer. About 300 times the actual age of the earth!

The intricacies of the human eye or the interplay of muscle, bone, tendons and nerves in a baby's hand point to a powerful designer. Even Charles Darwin himself, the originator of the theory of evolu-tion, wrote in his book *The Origin of the Species*, "To suppose that the eye, with so many parts all working together…could have been formed by natural selection (evolution), seems, I freely confess, absurd in the highest degree." He's right.

3. **The order of the universe.** Considering the earth alone, we see an incredible combination of factors that allow life to exist. If it were much larger, the earth's atmosphere would be unlivable; any smaller and it wouldn't exist at all. Even a small change in

the earth's distance from the sun would cause the fragile balance of the earth, and all life on it, to turn to ice or be incinerated. The tilt on its axis causes the rhythm of earth's seasons.

Examining the smallest components of energy reveals ever more examples of particles that exist in harmony, counter-balancing one another. There is order in all that is around us—the seen and the unseen. Just recently scientists discovered the Higgs boson, called "The God Particle, " which they predicted *must* exist in order for creation to demonstrate the awesome complexity it does.

4. ***The universe had a beginning.*** At one time it was thought that the universe had no beginning and was eternal. As recently as 50 years ago the theory of a "continuous creation" was assumed true.

Scientists have since learned that the universe experienced a distinct beginning through a sudden, cataclysmic release of energy. They call it the "Big Bang Theory." Most Christians call it Creation. The Bible says, "In the beginning you (God) laid the foundations of the earth, and the heavens are the work of your hands" (Psalms 102:25).

Even Dr. Robert Jastrow, founder of NASA's Institute for Space Studies, who calls himself an agnostic, says, "Now we see how the astronomical evidence points to a biblical view of the origin of the world. The details differ, but the essential elements are the same." As we understand the universe better, it points to the Creator.

5. ***The moral argument.*** There is a sense of right and wrong in all cultures. Laws are established to encourage what is right; consequences punish those who do wrong. Although there are exceptions, the great majority of civilizations have followed a similar code of what is good—courage, honesty, generosity, and what is bad—murder, theft, greed.

All peoples seem to have a similar inner sense of what is right or wrong. Without a Creator behind these concepts, if humans did develop from random chemical reactions, why would morals exist at all? It would make sense for people to behave in whatever way is in their self-interest, not in the interest of others.

Instead, we agree to follow certain values. In fact, the literature and mythology of most cultures throughout history has revered the most heroic of actions a human can take—sacrificing his or her life for another person. Why do we honor values that uplift others? Because God placed them in our hearts.

6. **Changed lives.** We see evidence of God in the way men and women change when they come to trust in Jesus Christ. Addictions have been healed, relationships restored, terrible offenses have been forgiven, and people sacrifice their desires for the benefit of others.

Humanly speaking, this doesn't make sense. Aside from God we should pursue whatever our emotions dictate. But when people allow God to enter their lives, they are miraculously changed. Sometimes dramatically, sometimes gradually, we are "transformed by the renewing of (our) minds" (Romans 12:2). Our own lives are evidence of God at work.

WHAT IS GOD LIKE?

We have looked at just a few examples of how our lives and the world around us proclaim that God lives. But what kind of God is he? Is he angry and fierce? Is he kind, but distant? Is he the least bit interested in us and in our concerns?

God is Infinite. He is utterly limitless. We humans are finite; we have limits to our strength, knowledge, goodness and our life itself. We have boundaries. God has none. All that he is, is without end. He is absolutely limitless!

God is One. The Bible tells us that God exists in three "Persons:" God the Father, God the Son and God the Holy Spirit. Each is distinct and has a unique role in the life of Christians, yet each works in perfect unity with the others. This attribute of God is difficult for us to understand. Because we are finite our understanding is limited. We believe this about God by faith, because his Word says it is true.

God is Eternal. God is not physical like humans; he is spiritual. Therefore, he isn't limited by space or time. God always was in the past, and he will always be in the future. In the Bible, God sometimes calls himself "I am." That means he is without beginning and without end. This, too, is so far beyond human experience that we can hardly understand it. Someday when we are in heaven, we'll understand completely.

> God is totally pure and completely without sin

God is Omniscient, Omnipresent and Omnipotent. We already said God is limitless; here we are specifically saying he knows everything (omniscient); there is nothing that is hidden from God. He is present everywhere (omnipresent); all people, all over the world, are under his watchful eye at all times. He is also all-powerful (omnipotent); his strength is beyond anything imaginable; it is without limit.

God is Holy and Good. God is totally pure and is completely without sin. There is no trace of evil in God; in other words, he is totally good. He is loving, kind, forgiving and patient. He endures all of our shortcomings and all of our selfishness because he loves us without end.

He is perfect and righteous and someday, he will punish those who reject his son, Jesus Christ. But his desire is that no one will die spiritually. For that reason, he continues to wait until everyone who will come to him has done so.

What a wonderful, magnificent God we have! We only have a glimpse of all that he is, but even that is indescribable. No wonder we can worship God and submit to his authority. Like David, we say, "Be exalted, O God, above the heavens, and let your glory be over all the earth" (Psalms 108:5).

Resources used in this section:
> *Handbook of Christian Apologetics*, by Peter Kreeft and Ronald K. Tacelli
> *A Ready Defense*, by Josh McDowell
> *Know What You Believe*, by Paul Little

Bible passage to read together:
    Psalm 8 - God is majestic
    Psalm 19 - All Creation declares God's existence
    Psalm 139 - God is all-knowing, all-present, all-powerful

Movies to watch together:
    Amazing Grace
    The Lord of the Rings Trilogy
    Bruce Almighty
    Evan Almighty
    God's Not Dead

Just about any movie that includes themes about God may leave us unsatisfied. Consider watching these, then discussing what you agreed or disagreed with, and what impact faith had on the main characters.

DISCUSSION QUESTIONS

Dad and Son:

1. What is it about God that is hard for you to comprehend? When you picture God, what kinds of characteristics come to your mind?

2. Is there anything about God that's hard for you to be thankful for?

3. In what ways does your view of God remind you of your dad? Do you need to change your view? Tell God how you feel about him. Be honest, he can take it.

4. If you have attached characteristics to God that are more like some men you have known, confess that to him.

Read Psalm 89:1-18 out loud. Thank God for the characteristics you admire about him.

 # JESUS SAVES

Jesus Christ, God's Son, is the central figure in the history of the world. This is reflected, for example, by the fact that much of the world follows a calendar based on the years he was on earth. Much more important though, Jesus is the Savior of mankind. It is only through him that we have acceptance in God's eyes.

When God created men and women he wanted companions whom he could love and who could love him in return. But he gave them the freedom to choose whether or not to love and obey him.

When, in the Garden of Eden, Adam and Eve were challenged by the serpent (Satan) to ignore God's instructions by eating the fruit of a forbidden tree, they failed God's trust. They disregarded God's warning and chose to defy him. At that moment their relationship with God was destroyed and the course of the story of mankind was forever changed.

Because all humans have followed Adam and Eve in sin, we no longer deserve to spend eternity in a perfect place (heaven) with a perfect God. Romans 3:23 says, "All have sinned and fall short of the glory of God." Even the best people can't measure up to God's standards of righteousness.

> **God provided a way for us to restore our broken relationship with him**

If that were an end of the story, we would all be doomed to an eternity separated from God in hell. Fortunately, God provided a way for us to restore our broken relationship with him, at a huge cost—the death of his son! John 3:16 tells us that "God so loved the world that he gave his one and only Son, that whoever believes in him shall not perish but have eternal life."

Jesus, the only perfectly sinless man in history, took the punishment we deserve for our sins: One sacrifice, for all people, for all time. Our sinfulness requires punishment, but God provides us eternal salvation if we place our trust in Christ. "For the wages (consequences) of sin is death, but the gift of God is eternal life in Christ Jesus our Lord" (Romans 6:23).

If we admit that we can't earn our way to heaven, that we can only return to a relationship with God through Jesus, and that he alone is our source of salvation, we are forgiven and pure in God's eyes.

We have no other hope; there is no other way to heaven. Jesus himself said, "I am the way, the truth and the life. No one comes to the Father except through me" (John 14:6).

This is not a decision that has to be made over and over. When we believe it and express that belief in God, we are saved. Once and for all! The eternal destination of our soul has changed forever. Jesus assures us: "I tell you the truth, whoever hears my word and believes him who sent me has eternal life and will not be condemned, he has crossed over from death to life" (John 5:24).

If you have made this decision in your heart, Jesus is already your Savior! If you have never done so, you will never face a more important choice the rest of your life. He longs to be your Savior, too. Is there any reason why you can't make that choice today? Do it! You'll never regret it.

Bible passages to read together:
John 3:16 - God loves the world
John 5:24 - Whoever hears Jesus' words will have eternal life
John 14:6 - Jesus is the Way
Romans 3:23, 24 - All fall short and are freely justified
Romans 6:23 - God's gift is eternal life

Movies to watch together:
The Gospel of John
The Passion of the Christ

DISCUSSION QUESTIONS

Dad and Son:
1. Have you accepted Christ as your Savior? If not, why not discuss this with a friend, a pastor or one of your Passage leaders this week?

2. Share with each other the story of how you became a Christian. How old were you? Where were you when it happened? Did someone explain the Gospel to you, or were you alone?

3. What other family members are Christians? Are there any that aren't? Consider praying together for them.

4. Since you became a Christian, what changes have you noticed in your life? What areas do you believe you need to continue to grow in?

5. In what ways would you like to continue to grow?

 ## DISCOVERING YOUR MISSION

One of the strongest desires of a man is to know what his purpose, or calling, in life is. Another word for this is "Mission." The old TV show your dad remembers, and the recent movies you remember, called *Mission: Impossible*, have a strong draw for men. That's what made them blockbuster hits.

Both words from that phrase hit a man's heart: first, *Mission*. The movie wasn't called *Experience: Impossible* or *Job: Impossible*. Those wouldn't have carried the same interest factor at all. Mission conveys an image of a challenge, something terrifically important, an adventure. It describes something bigger than the participants themselves that will require bravery, initiative and perseverance. A man longs to be part of a Mission.

The second word that hits men is *Impossible*. Again, they could have called it something like *Mission: Pretty Difficult* or *Mission: Piece of Cake*. Those probably wouldn't have worked very well. The mission was *impossible*! Really, really hard. It wasn't just some mundane job that needed to get done and didn't take much effort.

There was a message in the heart of Tom Cruise's movie character, and deep in every man's heart, that responds, "Impossible? Oh, yeah? We'll see." There is a deep desire in men to rise to the occasion, to be a hero in a larger-than-life story, to win despite insurmountable odds. A man wants to be on a mission that matters, one where winning won't be easy.

There's a problem, however. There is another message in men's hearts. This one is beneath the surface, and as a result, sounds louder. It says, "You? On a mission? Yeah, right. What do you think you have to offer? The only things you get excited about are the NFL and video games. Stay safe in your man cave or on your couch."

Most men hear that voice and, sadly, it drowns out the deeper truer voice that urges them to believe in something deeply enough that they'd be willing to die for it. They live life with a vague sense that they are missing out on something significant. They have lost "passion."

Even Satan has a purpose: "The thief's purpose is to kill and steal and destroy" (John 10:10). So what is God's purpose/ mission statement? "All things happen for good for those who love the Lord and are called according to *his purpose*" (Romans 8:28). What is God's purpose as is stated in the very next verse? "God chose us to become like his Son, so that his Son would be the first born with many brothers" (Romans 8:29).

God is in the process of transforming our hearts so that we become more like Christ—yes even brothers of Christ—sharing the same Father. Wow! What an identity. What a heritage. What a legacy.

We are adopted into the same Father-Son relationship that Christ has. Yet this is a process of becoming holy—a saint—and living out the mission for which we were created through a process called sanctification. And the good news is that he orchestrates this process if we let God have his way with us by being willing to give up everything to him, "no matter the cost" (see Luke 14:25-33).

As this occurs, we become more like Christ, and even a brother of Christ: "So now Jesus and the ones he makes holy have the same Father. That is why Jesus is not ashamed to call them his brothers" (Hebrews 2:11).

As we become more like Christ, our hearts will desire to fulfill Christ's mission statement: Jesus said, "He has sent me to proclaim that the captives will be released, that the blind will see, that the downtrodden will be freed from their oppressors, and that the time of the Lord's favor has come!" (Luke 4:18-19). Further, Christ said his purpose was to be "a King" (John 18:37).

> *Our life mission is always for the benefit of others*

As we become brothers of Christ—joining him in the Royal Family—our hearts' desire will be to help "set the captives free:" to be rescuers of people who are in desperate need, whether physically, emotionally or spiritually.

What does it look like to join Christ in his mission to set the captives free? Throughout Scripture Jesus further describes his mission. He said, "I have come to find and to save anyone who is lost." "I haven't come to be served, instead I came to serve others." " I have come so others can have real life, and have it abundantly." These were his words to people who were fearful and doubtful; people who eventually rejected him and killed him in the most painful manner known to man. He tried to serve those who hated him. That was a Mission: Impossible.

Each of us has a shared quality in our life mission. *It is always for the benefit of others.* In fact, that is the essence of a true mission. An assignment that is for our own benefit may be an assignment or a goal or a dream. But a mission is always directed toward others in need.

Jesus prays to his Father for his followers, saying: "As you sent me into the world, I have sent them into the world" (John 17:18). It's a mission that he gives only to us because it is defined by our unique gifts, talents, values and life-experiences.

Before exploring what our personal unique mission is, it's important to realize that all of us who call ourselves brothers of Jesus Christ have two missions we share with each other. These have been pointed out by Richard Bolles in his excellent booklet entitled, *Finding Your Mission in Life:*

1. *To have an increasing awareness of God's presence with us and around us, every moment of our lives.* God is sovereign; his presence is everywhere. Some people like to describe a miraculous situation as being one where "God showed up." No, this is a poor perspective. God is already there long before we are. It is WE who finally show up and acknowledge God's powerful presence in our lives. Living with this awareness, regardless of our circumstances is our first mission.

2. *To live our lives in such a way that we bring the Spirit of Christ with us in every relationship and encounter we have.* In the battles that we will face, we need God with us through his Spirit in order to do the powerful work of the Father. Even Jesus said, "I assure you, the Son can do nothing by himself. He does only what he sees the Father doing" (John 5:19).

Wouldn't it be wonderful if we were increasingly the kind of men who, when we arrive in any situation, we bring an undeniable spirit about us? A spirit that is both confident and humble, both compassionate and courageous. We can; it's the Holy Spirit who already lives in us. We have a mission to live in submission to that Spirit—to follow Christ unconditionally.

OUR UNIQUE, PERSONAL MISSION

Having understood that these first two missions are lifelong callings that all Christians share, we can explore *our personal mission.* Discovering this mission is extremely important. It opens our eyes to a deeper level of meaning for our lives.

How does a man discover his mission? It's hard; it takes time and effort. That's why most men never find it. Earlier we quoted Emerson as saying, "The majority of men live lives of quiet desperation..." Some resources attribute the rest of his quote as being, "...and go to the grave without singing their song."

Whether he actually said the remainder of that quote or not, it is still stunning in its truth. Most men DO go to the grave never having sung their song, never having discovered and lived out their mission in life. Most men don't even know there *is* a song they can sing. It's why we see so many men who DO lead lives of quiet desperation.

There are many clues about your mission you can pick up through life, "should you decide to accept it."

- When you read stories as a boy did you identify with a certain character or hero? Did you want to be like him? What was it about him that you admired? That identification is a clue to the kind of attributes or impact that are important to you.
- What did you dream about becoming when "you grew up?" Do you still have that dream? The qualities of that kind of job, or a man who can accomplish that kind of task, are a further clue to your mission.
- Did you ever watch a movie and feel a surge of emotion building up in your chest that made you think you might explode? Perhaps you felt like cheering, or yelling, or maybe even felt like crying. Those emotions are revealing something important about your heart. That passion brought to the surface is a window to the issues that stir your heart.
- Perhaps you've had someone tell you, "You know, you are really good at music!" Or, "I can tell you really enjoy kids. Have you ever thought about being a teacher some day?" Other people often have observations about your abilities or impact that you aren't aware of. Those are clues to your mission.

Below are further questions for thought and conversation that can help you get started in identifying the unique role God had in mind for you when he made you. Dads and sons, talk them through, help each other think through possible answers, and see what they reveal about your missions.

Bible passages to read together:
    Luke 4: 18, 19 - Jesus' profound calling
    John 17 - Jesus reveals his mission, and blesses us in ours
    Romans 8: 28, 29 - God has a purpose in mind for us

Movie to watch together:
    Glory (especially scene 27)
    The Mission

DISCUSSION QUESTIONS

Dad:

1. Have you ever identified principles that are deeply important to you? Do you know what impact you consistently have in the lives of others?

2. What do you already see in your son that might be clues to his mission?

Son:

1. Do you have any ideas what your dad's mission is?

Dad and Son:

1. What are your favorite movies? What is it about the movie that stirs you? Who is your favorite character? What does he believe in, and what impact does he have?

2. What do you want to change about the world or about our society? What makes you angry?

3. Who are your favorite role models or heroes in real life? What do you admire about them?

4. Is there a group of people that you care about deeply; people you would like to help if you could?

Record your observations in three categories:
1. *Actions or Talents* that express action that you like to take.

Examples of action words: Launch, Empower, Challenge, Inspire, Encourage, Model, Demonstrate, Organize, Order, Produce, Simplify, Increase, Defend, Expand, Protect, Discover, Serve, Teach, Support, Build, Release, Liberate, Promote, Communicate, Write, Connect, Strengthen, Create, Sing, Equip, Unify, Train, Repair, Guide

Circle one or two of these Talents that you consistently bring into any situation.

2. *Principles or Values* that are unusually important to you.

Examples of values words: Freedom, Excellence, Hope, Integrity, Dreams, Passion, Healing, Truth, Compassion, Dignity, Value, Self Esteem, Harmony, Purpose, Order, Beauty, Honor, Nobility, Loyalty, Service, Meaning, Love, Strength, Justice, Faithfulness, Intimacy, Courage, Respect, Life, Joy, Honesty, Humility, Wisdom, Kindness, Inspiration, Salvation, Protection, Comfort, Victory, Health, Worship, Generosity, Perseverance

Circle one or two of these Values that inspire and motivate you.

3. The kind of *People* you care about, or might like to help.

Examples of people groups: Poor, Sick, Families, Leaders, Children, Athletes, Men/Women, The Church, Orphans, Oppressed, Needy, Parents, Homeless, Students, Business people, Hungry, Refugees, Imprisoned, Widows, Singles, Confused, Desperate, Endangered, Wealthy, Successful, Teens, Spiritually Lost, Hopeless, Rejected, Unpopular, Strangers, Internationals, Unemployed, Frightened, Neighbors, Defenseless, Teachers

Circle one or two of these People groups that you have unusual compassion for.

Dads and sons, work together, and separately, over time to narrow down your thoughts to one talent, one value and one type of person that means the most to you. Then combine them in a sentence in a pattern like this:

My mission is to (verb) (value or belief) to (person or group).

For example:
My mission is to <u>bring hope</u> to <u>homeless people</u>.
Or:
My Mission is to <u>inspire</u> a <u>joy for learning</u> in <u>Middle School students</u>.
(Perhaps another Mission: Impossible!)

Craig's mission is
To guide and inspire men on their life journey, to help them pass on a life-giving legacy.

Jesus' said his mission was:
To <u>bring abundant life</u> to <u>those who are lost.</u>

Don't feel like you have to figure this out perfectly or quickly. Remember most men never discover the secret of their Mission. Put some thought to it; talk about it with each other; put something in writing; and let it grow over time. You'll be glad you did.

NOTES

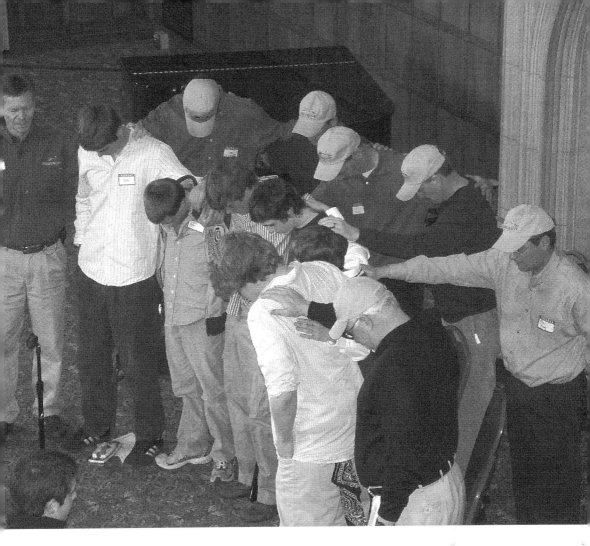

 # CELEBRATION CEREMONY

Following the completion of the Passage to Manhood program we urge dads to organize two more important components:

1. **A Celebration Ceremony** where each father-son pair can share with moms, siblings, pastors and friends what they learned from the experience.

2. **An adventure** that dads and sons plan and complete together. Both of these events serve to mark the Passage experience in a way that cements its significance and memory.

Below is a suggested pattern for the Celebration Ceremony followed by examples of adventures dads and sons might want to share together.

BLESSING AND CELEBRATION WITH FAMILY AND FRIENDS

I. **Welcome to family and guests** (Passage leader or dad)

II. **Sharing about the Passage experience** (fathers and sons together)

Dads give your comments on the following:
- Why did you want to experience this program with your son?
- What was the most significant discovery or experience for you?
- What Mission Statement have you identified?

Sons give your comments on the following:
- What part did you enjoy the most?
- What is an important lesson you learned about manhood?
- What Mission Statement have you identified?
- Tell what adventure you and your father will be taking: when and where.

III. **Blessing** (sons, dads and moms in front of others)

Optional: Mother and/or special guest give words of blessing to the son

Required: Fathers speak a blessing to their sons. As a guideline consider two ideas:

1. What would you have wanted to hear your father say about you in public?
2. Follow the model that God spoke of Jesus: Identification of sonship, expression of love, expression of pride, identify a specific character quality or gift you admire in him.

Keep comments to three minutes or less.

Sample comment:

Alexander McLean Glass, your mother and I named you for your great, great grandfather who is buried in a small church cemetery on the coast of Northern Ireland. He was a man of God; he was a part of your story.

We also gave you the name, Alexander, because it means: Defender of Men. We dedicated you as a child to God, knowing that you were a blessed gift to us, shared with us to raise you to glorify God and to serve mankind.

Alec, I see God at work in you as a young man. You are compassionate, you have a wonderful sense of humor, and you are deeply perceptive. You also have chosen to be a Christ follower when you dedicated yourself to the Lord when you were five. You have brought Mom and me great joy.

Alec, today it is my privilege as your father, to honor you in front of our family and friends. Son, I love you; I am proud of you; I thank God that he gave you to me. Today I call you out to join me in this community of men. From this day on I will always respect you as a man."

IV. **Presentation of gifts** (certificates and compasses)

It usually works best for dads to agree on a common gift that they will all give to each of their sons in the public ceremony. This avoids the awkwardness of one dad giving his son an engraved broadsword, while another gives him a pen and pencil set. A classic styled metal compass with the son's name engraved on the inside serves as a symbolic, personal and affordable gift.

V. Celebration dessert (Each family bring enough to feed ten)

VI. Prayer of dedication (Pastor or Passage leader)

CERTIFICATE OF Achievement

THIS IS TO CERTIFY THAT

HAS SUCCESSFULLY COMPLETED THE

PASSAGE TO MANHOOD

AS CONFIRMED BY A COMMUNITY OF MEN

AT _____

DATE _____

GUIDE _____

FATHER _____

Sample certificate of completion

 # FATHER/SON ADVENTURE

Purpose

For the father and son to plan a memorable adventure and then experience that adventure together within the next three or four months. It should include an activity or challenge that allows the young man to demonstrate a trait of adulthood (e.g., creativity, courage, responsibility.) When completed, this experience will be a reminder of the young man's emerging role and responsibility as part of the community of men.

Plan

Begin planning now. The young man can do most of the research. Fathers should guide him in picking something that will have special meaning to him (and you). **The son should be prepared to present a report of your planned adventure at the Celebration Ceremony.**

Ideas to consider:

Outdoors
- ▸ backpacking/camping
- ▸ white-water rafting
- ▸ wilderness survival
- ▸ biking Trip

Sports
- ▸ special ball game
- ▸ Tough Mudder or Spartan challenge race
- ▸ pro-sports camp, i.e. baseball, NASCAR
- ▸ learn something new together; e.g., martial arts, riflery, bow shooting, etc.

Cultural
- ▸ symphony
- ▸ arts
- ▸ do a creative project together

Travel
- ▸ special country of heritage
- ▸ trip to another part of the U.S.
- ▸ adventurous location

Go with a group
- ▸ Summit Adventures
- ▸ Outward Bound
- ▸ Short-term missions trip

(Adventure concepts developed in partnership with Gentry Gardner of Sure Passage.)

ABOUT CRAIG GLASS

Craig has had a variety of ministry roles throughout his career. He spent 20 years with International Teams, first leading a team based in Vienna, smuggling Christian literature behind the Iron Curtain, then as Vice President of Ministries providing leadership training and pastoral support to 400 staff world-wide.

From 1995 through 1999 Craig served on the staff of Willow Creek Community Church as a leader of the Legacy men's ministry, consisting of 100 small groups and 800 men.

The following three years Craig served as National Director and Vice President of Team Ministries with International Students Inc., with responsibilities for the oversight of the national and regional directors.

Currently Craig is the Founder/President of Peregrine Ministries International whose vision is to guide and inspire men on their life journey, to help them pass on a life-giving legacy. Through personalized one-on-one coaching, small group leadership and inspirational speaking, Craig has helped countless men gain a clearer sense of their purpose and the legacy they want to leave in the lives of others.

Craig and his wife Beryl live in Monument, Colorado. They have been married for more than 40 years, have three children and five grandchildren.

In his free time Craig enjoys competitive swimming, mountain biking, hiking, golf and reading.

About Peregrine Ministries

Our mission: We guide and inspire men on their life journey, to help them pass on a life-giving legacy.

Our vision: To see a growing community of men who:
- understand their identity is in Christ
- embrace their roles as men
- live out the personal calling God has for their lives

We come alongside men *individually*, in *small groups* and in *large retreats*, helping them identify their true priorities and then live their lives accordingly.

One of our favorite things to do is to *partner with churches* to help them identify, establish and develop their own vision for their men. We encourage you to let your church pastor or men's ministry leader know of the mission and impact of Peregrine. We'd love to explore the possibilities of partnering with your church.

We invite you to check out, subscribe to, or like the following:
Website: **www.peregrineministries.org**
Men Matter blog: **www.craigglass.org**
Men Matter Facebook page: **www.facebook.com/menmatter.craigglass**
Men Matter radio: **www.menmattertoday.com**

Made in the USA
Middletown, DE
21 May 2018